ARCHITECTURE
FOR THE
BOOKS

MICHAEL J. CROSBIE

First published in Australia in 2003 by
The Images Publishing Group Pty Ltd
ABN 89 059 734 431
6 Bastow Place, Mulgrave, Victoria, 3170, Australia
Telephone: +61 3 9561 5544 Facsimile: +61 3 9561 4860
Email: books@images.com.au
Website: www.imagespublishinggroup.com

Copyright © The Images Publishing Group Pty Ltd
The Images Publishing Group Reference Number: 441

National Library of Australia
Cataloguing-in-Publication data

Crosbie, Michael J. (Michael James).
Architecture for the Books.

ISBN: 1 876907 49 5

1. Library architecture. I. Title.

727.8

Coordinating Editor: Sarah Noal
Designed by The Graphic Image Studio Pty Ltd,
Mulgrave, Australia
Film by Ocean Graphic Company Limited
Printed by Max Production Printing & Book-binding Limited

IMAGES has included on its website a page for special notices in
relation to this and our other publications. Please visit this site:
www.imagespublishinggroup.com

Preface
What is a Library?

Information is the new currency of our age. The book you are holding is unlike most household objects, in that there is a building, perhaps within walking distance that was specially designed and constructed to give it a home. Like the monasteries of the Middle Ages, the library is an outpost of civilization in any community. Along with the town hall, the school, the church, and the bank, the library became an essential ingredient in the establishment of any town. Branch libraries are like big, friendly houses in the neighborhood, always welcoming and often full of unexpected pleasures.

Libraries are not simply places where books live when they're not being thumbed through. In large cities and small towns alike, the library is simultaneously a setting for self-motivated scholars and a haven for dreamers. How many of us have occupied the far end of an aisle in the book stacks, sitting cross-legged on the floor with a volume on our lap, traveling on the wings of a book? Libraries are places where you can lose yourself among the pages, in music, reading the paper, catching up on gossip. In many small towns, the library continues to serve as the social anchor. For example, consider the Friend Memorial Library in this book. Its scale is domestic and comfortable, taking its place in a town like many of the old frame houses that line the streets of Brooklin, Maine. You can imagine on any given afternoon the casual swapping of town news and whispered outrage about some perceived indiscretion by a pillar of the community. The library, as a social center, is as often a setting for the exchange of oral history and late-breaking news as it is a repository of books and tapes.

On the other end of the scale, libraries sometimes take on the role of cultural centers, holding within their walls the very identity of a nation or a people. A good example of this is the Bibliotheca Alexandrina in Egypt. Historically, this building is the heir to the Great Library of Alexandria, which burned down in 48 BC. The new library assumes the mantle of the old and is a library of international significance. The sense of space perceived in its voluminous reading room seems to capture that stature in three dimensions. It is a fitting example of how space itself is used to communicate a sense of importance.

Versatility is a watchword in library design. There are a number of libraries in this book that serve universities and research centers. Because of the critical importance of the word in teaching and scholarship, these buildings are often quite literally at the center of the academic world—physically and symbolically. The library has traditionally been the place where students and scholars come together, not only to exchange information, but also to socialize and to share the culture of the institution.

Electronic access to information globally means that the new library never shuts its doors. Many of the university libraries included here are open 24 hours a day, and serve as a home away from the dorm for students. The John Deaver Drinko Library at Marshall University, for example, is less a repository for books than a portal for accessing information in all of its varied forms. It has 26 networked study rooms (most of them with computer terminals), 'collaboration rooms' with teleconferencing capabilities, data ports in the lounge for students to plug their laptops into, an electronic training room, electronic document delivery systems, and a multimedia collection that is Web-accessible (there are about 800 data ports throughout the building). Right next to the front door is a 24-hour reading room and café. Drinko is a pointer to the university library of the future, where social exchange and access to collections in other libraries worldwide will be commonplace.

Sustainability reflects a larger movement in architecture, and libraries can teach about it in many ways. Buildings such as the South Jamaica Branch Library and the Langston Hughes Library communicate the value of sustainability and conservation in the built environment. Greater reliance on natural lighting to reduce energy consumption, recycled and recyclable materials and building products, passive heating and cooling systems, and better indoor air quality are just some of the strategies used in these libraries. As important community resources, libraries have a valuable role to play as examples of responsible and socially conscious design, construction, and building operation. They can become teaching instruments that demonstrate the techniques and values of conserving natural resources.

Communities risk the loss of identity through every new building they undertake. All buildings, and libraries in particular, have a role to play here as well. The library can serve not only as a repository of books, but also as a vessel of history and cultural values. How is this possible?

One way is for the architecture to recall the character of the region. For example, the Evanston Public Library captures some of the spirit of Frank Lloyd Wright's Prairie-style architecture in its repetitive and ornate column capitals framing clerestory windows, and in its slab-like masses (which have some of the flavor of Wright's Unity Temple in Oak Park, Illinois).

Unsung architecture is also worthy of emulation. One sees such an approach in the Timberland North Mason Public Library in Belfair, Washington. Here, the architect has used humble exterior materials such as concrete block and ribbed metal wall and roof cladding to conjure local mill building construction. The interior's large timber trusses, over the reading room and circulation spine, are reminiscent of a mill-run shed—a common vernacular building in this part of the world.

Taken as a refuge for dreamers, the library can be a record of their dreams. The project in this book that best exemplifies this is the Los Feliz Branch Library in Los Angeles. The pyramidal ceiling of one of the library spaces is covered with a public artwork, *The Conjunction of 500 Wishes*, which was worded with the help of those who live in the neighborhood and use the library daily. Over one's head, in a labyrinthine maze of spirals and zigzags, are rendered the hopes and dreams of those for whom the library is a welcoming refuge.

Michael J. Crosbie

Contents

Introduction
Designing the Contemporary Library

Our historically romantic notion of the library is that of mellow book-lined walls creating discrete places for reading, browsing, and study; the book defining the architecture. Such a mental image is valid for good reason. The book defining the space of architecture has a long history. In medieval monastic libraries, book-lined cabinets or cells provided individual study spaces within greater structures. The 1475 painting, *St Jerome in his Study* by Antonello da Messina,[1] illustrates this beautifully. In baroque monastic libraries, sensuous walls and piers of books created fluid spaces with the carefully controlled natural light to dramatic effect.[2] In Etienne-Louis Boullée's drawings of 1785 for the enormous reading room of the Bibliothèque du Roi, Paris,[3] where the power of the collector is omnipresent, the walls are book-lined. In Paris, at the Bibliothèque Saint-Geneviève of 1850 and the Bibliothèque Nationale of 1868,[4] both by Henri Labrouste and both highly innovative in their use of light and application of structure, the walls are multi-tiered book ranges. In the US, at about the same time, H.H. Richardson, in his inventive Romanesque Revival mode, was making thick walls of stone, brick, and books.[5] As late as 1928, Gunnar Asplund was lining the great rotunda at the Stockholm Public Library[6] with books.

As rich and evocative as these examples are, it is not the environment of most contemporary libraries. As digital catalogs have taken the place of card catalogs, the computer, with patrons busily clicking and searching, is one of the first interior impressions of the library. The great benefits of the digital catalog, the dispersion of catalog information throughout the library, remote access to information, and the enhanced catalog search beyond the collection at hand, assure its status. More often than not, the tactile, visual contact with books is a third, fourth or fifth removed experience in the library's sequence of spaces and functions. With only the occasional exception, walls of books no longer make the space of the contemporary library. The San Juan Capistrano Public Library, in San Juan Capistrano, California of 1982 by Michael Graves[7] is one of the exceptions.

The storage of large collections, the advent of a numerical and linear cataloging system, and concerns for flexibility in the ever-changing library landscape have prompted the creation of large open areas filled with furniture. The quantities and locations of reading tables, carrels, shelving, and other furniture and equipment are manipulated to meet current and changing needs. Large open areas address the issue of security and supervision, particularly important in public libraries where patron safety is a concern and library staffing is frequently subject to fluctuating funds.

The architectural design challenge of large open spaces is two-fold: first, the articulation of such spaces can prove daunting at the very moment such spaces present architectural opportunities. The problem becomes more pronounced in stacked, multistory libraries than in single-story libraries, which have only the plane of the roof to address. A second significant challenge of large open undifferentiated space is the loss of intimate space for the individual to study or concentrate and interact personally with a book or computer. While furniture, in many cases, can solve this need, it is often relegated to bulk-purchasing programs or is procured under arrangements separate from the architect's purview. In such cases, the result is often disappointing and conceptually inconsistent with the space design.

There are, however, wonderful examples where furniture and architecture work together beautifully. At Louis I. Kahn's Library at Phillips Exeter Academy in Exeter, New Hampshire, 1972,[8] individual study carrels at the building's perimeter give scale, privacy, visual access to the exterior, and even the modulation of natural light to the user. Alvar Aalto often made similar furniture or furniture-like rooms. The spaces at the perimeter of his Mount Angel Abbey Library of 1970,[9] the monastic library at the Mount Angel Benedictine Monastery east of Mount Angel, Oregon, are an excellent example. More recently, Moshe Safdie's design for Library Square, comprised of Vancouver's Central Library and Federal Government Office Tower,[10] places patrons in intimate spaces at the library's perimeter overlooking the city.

In one 'future think' digital scenario, the personalized intimate space, in the form of the carrel or cabinet, could take on new life. One can imagine cabinets enhanced for exterior conditions or as portable mobile units. The carrel/cabinet could be dispersed across a library, a neighborhood, a city, or a region. In such a scenario, the dispersion of 'small public libraries,' or conglomerated cabinets could prove particularly important to those of us who are not able to personally acquire the software and/or hardware necessary to be adequately 'cyberized' or not able to amass personal book collections.

The free, public accessibility to computers, books, and other informational media is essential to any society that values freedom of thought and speech. Public libraries find and will continue to find creative and affordable ways to honor this mandate—the Jeffersonian ideal of the free library open to everyone.

continued

In the US, public libraries may be the only truly public buildings. Unlike private or academic libraries, public libraries generally serve widely diverse communities. As a result, the making of public libraries tends to be a complicated process. During the design of a public library, the community may be involved through public meetings established by law or instituted by the library system. In other cases, a library board or a committee may represent the community. County, city, or state entities may all be involved. In any combination or configuration of stakeholders, influencers, or decision makers the collective community personality registers itself on the building design through its attitude towards budget, program, leadership, and issues of architectural character. One example is the programmatic inclusion of public space. While a subset to the primary focus of the library, such spaces and their functions leave their mark on the plans and use-patterns of the building.

New technologies affecting library design are both architectonic and informational. Since the great tracery and buttress walls of the Gothic cathedrals, the trajectory of architectural tectonics has included the search for the thin or highly efficient wall. Thin walls have become a characteristic of modern/contemporary architecture. No longer of thick masonry, the thin wall resonates in the architecture of contemporary libraries in important ways and holds out the promise of elegant solutions in the future. Thin walls are constructed of glazing systems or of structural framing with exterior and interior veneers, both systems manufactured from parts and pieces often of close tolerances. Because the book has become disengaged from the wall, library buildings now act as 'tents' or cloaks around collections and the advanced technologies of thin walls equate to efficient enclosures.

The four bold glass towers of the National Library of France in Paris, 1995–96, by Dominique Perrault[11] clearly express the thin walls/large collection phenomenon. In contemporary revivalist or historicist architecture, the thin wall begs the question of authenticity. While often producing pleasing picturesque representations, such an approach seldom takes on the more productive task of the thin wall as a medium of exploration. As with examples from the past, the libraries that will be celebrated in the future will be those that have prompted and/or benefited from the continuing research of innovative structural systems, building materials, and techniques, and the exploration of architectural space. Architectural character born of such exploration signals the reinvention or evolution of the building type as well as the investment required to go beyond formulaic solutions. Architectural character is, in the final analysis, the aspect of great libraries that endear them to us and over time ensure their continued presence.

Light is a defining consideration for libraries. Whether natural or artificial, light is the key to access the treasures of the library—be it light from the computer screen or light that falls upon the page of an open book. The technologies of artificial lighting are constantly improving, allowing greater and greater flexibility of design approach. This is particularly important for very large collections where natural light is simply not a comprehensive option. In contemporary architecture, natural light is controlled and filtered by progressively more sophisticated and effective glazing materials and window treatment systems.

The search for the relationship or interface of digital or informational technologies with physical technologies will surely take architecture to places yet unpredictable. In a recent publication focusing on school design architect Sheila Kennedy commented, 'The physical world has not been "replaced" by the digital world, as once initially predicted. Instead, we are discovering that the digital world is increasingly absorbed into and merged with the physical world.'[12] It is fundamental that the human interface with either the book or the computer is based on the dimensions and capabilities of the human body and is wonderfully one of the 'givens' in the otherwise shifting project of architecture. The physical relationship of the individual to the computer is not so very different from the individual's relationship to a book, note once again St Jerome in his Study. New technology may enhance but will not diminish the need for the human dimension of the library. Until such time that information technology becomes integrated with our bodies, or our buildings, the space required to use a computer or to read a book remains constant and definable.[13]

The computer—while giving us access to enormous stores of information electronically—has, rather than producing a paperless society, facilitated an ever-increasing production of paper publication. Individuals may publish with ease in informal formats. In the US, the average number of books published annually in paper format over a four-year period from 1998–2001 was 119,049 volumes.[14] Although this may change radically in the future, the development of the e-book is presently considered a supplement to the traditional book. With the application of the computer, there is reason to believe that, in the future, even libraries themselves may generate or become the publishers of information.[15] The longevity of electronic storage continues as a consideration, and it is currently estimated that the amount of digitized information is only 10 percent of all text.[16] The feel of a book in our hands is comforting and hard copy is reassuring.

Libraries are the containers for and disseminators of information. Libraries gather our universes of understanding under a single roof. Even as the method of storage shifts into a digital format, two aspects remain constant. First, the library houses and makes accessible the apparatus of information transmission. Second, the library provides a place of socialization and collectivity. Socialization may be in the form of interaction with the librarian whose task it is to handle information and see that it gets to those desiring it, or it may be in the form of interaction of community, either scholarly or casual. The individual alone with either a book or a computer has limits. As social creatures, our need for human interaction is essential and inherent. The library building functions as a symbol of our collective belief in knowledge as the sustaining fiber of our culture and of our human civility. Even as the virtual library is being realized, the need for access to resources beyond our means and the need for human contact collectively drive the prediction of the library of the future not to an either/or condition, but rather to a both/and condition—both the electronic, virtual library and the library of space, light, and materiality. The merging of the virtual and the physical portend well for the continuing tradition of extraordinary developments in the architectural presence of libraries and the development of architectural character yet unfathomable.

Merrill Elam, Mack Scogin Merrill Elam Architects

Notes

1 Paul Crowther, *The Transhistorical Image: Philosophizing Art and Its History* (Cambridge University Press, Cambridge, 2002), 50.

2 Michael Brawne, *Libraries: Architecture and Equipment* (Praeger Publishers, New York, 1970), 14–15.

3 Philippe Madec, *Boullée* (Fernand Hazan, Paris, 1986), 90.

4 Spiro Kostof, *A History of Architecture: Settings and Rituals* (Oxford University Press, New York, 1985), 658.

5 Sir Banister Fletcher, *A History of Architecture on the Comparative Method* (Charles Scribner's Sons, New York, 1961), 1063–1064.

6 Claes Caldenby and Olof Hultin, *Asplund* (Arkitektur Förlag, Stockholm, 1985), 92–141.

7 John Pastier, 'An Intimate Sequence of Spaces,' *Architecture*, Dec. 1989, 64–67.

8 David B. Brownlee and David G. De Long, *Louis I. Kahn: In the Realm of Architecture* (Rizzoli International Publications, New York, 1991), 258–265.

9 David Dunster ed., *Alvar Aalto* (St Martin's Press, New York, 1978), 60–62.

10 Wendy Kohn ed., *Moshe Safdie* (Academy Editions, London, 1996), 284–301.

11 Michel Jacques ed., *Bibliothèque Nationale de France* (Birkhauser Verlag, Basel, 1996).

12 Sheila Kennedy, 'Something from "Nothing": Information Infrastructure in School Design,' *Schools for Cities, Urban Strategies*, ed. Sharon Haar (National Endowment for the Arts, Washington, DC, 2002), 45.

13 Paul Lukez, 'Whiter://Multi-media.(Cyber).Libraries?' *Library Builders*, ed., Michael Brawne (London: Academy Editorions, 1997), 13.

14 Dave Bogart, ed., *The Bowker Annual 2002*, 47th ed. (Medford, New Information Today, Inc, Jersey, 2002), 548.

15 Paul Lukez, 14.

16 Paul Lukez, 14.

PROJECTS

Projects

Bibliotheca Alexandrina

Snøhetta
Hamza Associates

Conceived as a revival of the ancient library in the city founded by Alexander the Great some 2300 years ago and lost to civilization centuries later, this new 85,000-square-meter library in Alexandria, Egypt is distinguished by its circular, tilting form. The building spans 160 meters in diameter and reaches up to 32 meters in height, while also diving some 12 meters into the ground. An open plaza and reflecting pool surrounds the building, and a footbridge links the city to the nearby University of Alexandria.

The library's circular form alongside the circular Alexandrian harbor recalls the cyclical nature of knowledge, fluid throughout time. Its tilting roof suggests the ancient Alexandrian lighthouse and provides the city with a new symbol for learning and culture. This grand edifice includes a 6000-square-meter stone wall carved with alphabetic inscriptions from around the world in a careful display of the library's basic proviso, language.

The 20,000-square-meter, 2000-seat open reading room, the largest of its kind in the world, occupies more than half of the library volume and is stepped over seven terraces. Indirectly lit by vertical, north-facing skylights in the roof, this space is not exposed to direct sunlight, harmful to books and manuscripts. Reading areas and stacks are arranged at close proximity at the same level, the stacks being placed at each terrace level, underneath the next higher terrace. Readers sitting at the terrace edge enjoy maximum exposure to natural light and grand views of the space while being in close proximity to book storage. This concept is repeated throughout the room and creates a large amphitheater with a wide variety of evenly lit reading facilities. The 11-story library can contain up to 4 million volumes with conventional shelf storage, and 8 million with the use of compact storage.

continued

1 Library from northeast, with its dramatic, curved stone wall

2 Conference area has gently arced wall

3 View of lower level of planetarium

4 Detail of stone wall, inscribed with different alphabets

In addition to the library facilities, the Bibliotheca also contains a planetarium, several museums, a school for information science, conservation facilities, and a young person's library. A new conference center linked to an existing auditorium on the site makes the Bibliotheca a centerpiece for both learning and debate.

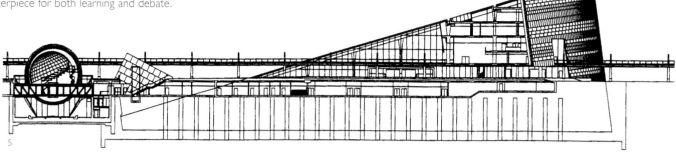

5

6

7

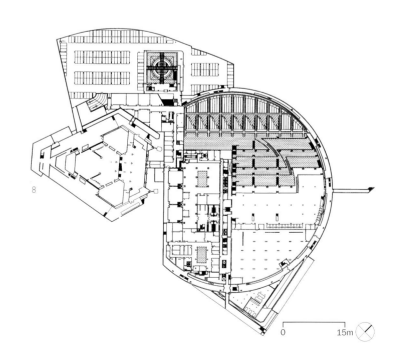

8

5 Section

6 Multistory reading areas in main reading room

7 Ceiling's pyramidal forms allow filtered light

8 Fourth floor plan—one of library's 11 different stories

opposite: Reading room is one large space with seating for 2000

photography: Gerald Zugman

0   15m

Friend Memorial Library

Elliott & Elliott Architecture

1

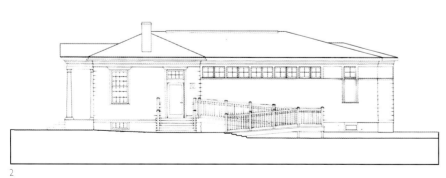

2

The Friend Memorial Library, housed in a 1912 colonial-revival building on a wooded site in Brooklin, Maine met its need for expansion by replacing an unsound earlier addition with 1400 square feet of well-ordered space. Keeping the warm and humble atmosphere appropriate for a small coastal Maine town library, the architects worked with the library director and a five-person committee to design an open, flexible interior within a modest construction budget.

The exterior details remain virtually the same, and the library maintains its classical architecture bearing in the community. One enters on axis through the columned portico. Once through the airlock entry (common in Maine's harsh climate), one arrives at the lobby and circulation desk, which is directly on axis with the entry. Reading areas with bookshelves are found to the left and right of the desk. Beyond the circulation desk is more stack space in one large room.

To preserve the concept of the original 'one-room' library, the central low stacks are mounted on casters and roll into the tall outer stacks. This allows the center of the room to be cleared for presentations and lectures. The space can accommodate assemblies of up to 60 people. The addition of plentiful natural light, large windows overlooking surrounding woods, and an elegant circulation desk crafted by a local boat builder enhances the library's presence.

As the central hub of the library, the circulation desk is the crossroads of the space. Interior glass windows deliver natural light throughout the building, and promote views from one area to another. This makes the space appear expansive and seem more generous than it actually is.

3

4   5   6

1 Circulation desk as one enters library; note cork flooring

2 Side elevation

3 Exterior of library has strong domestic scale

4 Stacks on casters allow room to be used for large gatherings

5 Light colors and built-in bookshelves in reading area

6 Detail of card catalog

photography: Smalling Photography

Morgan Library
Colorado State University

Perry Dean Rogers | Partners Architects
Luis O. Acosta (Associate Architect)

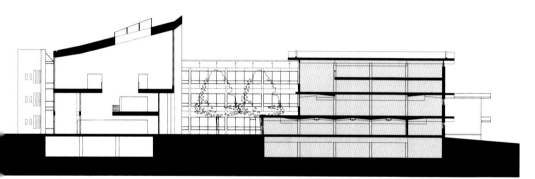

The Morgan Library at Colorado State University (CSU) in Fort Collins, Colorado was built in the 1960s, with an L-shaped plan flanking two sides of a plaza at the southern edge of the campus. The main entrance was located at the intersection of the 'L' making it difficult to use, and modest in scale. Collections stored on either side of the entrance had expanded into reading areas, and wiring was incomplete.

The university's master plan called for a single addition to the western side of the building, overlooking the front range of the Rocky Mountains. The program was dissected into two so that the issues presented by the entrance and plaza could be addressed by adding a second 'L' on the plaza itself, to which the main entrance could be relocated.

The architects added an outdoor reading courtyard at the center of the plan, as well as storage capacity and additional reading space in a second wing along the western edge.

Adjacent open space, nearby buildings, and pedestrian or vehicular requirements influenced each part of the composition. The scale of the components varies depending on the distance from which the building is perceived, so that the completed building acts to knit together the campus fabric in an urbanistic manner.

The materials used are yellow and ochre sandstone, quarried locally and found on most of the buildings at CSU, aluminum curtainwall, and exposed concrete. The building houses 1,500,000 volumes and accommodates 2600 readers.

2

4

5

3

1 Section
2 Wall of entry curves to welcome visitors
3 Multistory space provides orientation
4 Natural stone is drawn from indigenous sources
5 Obverse of curved natural stone wall

6

7

8

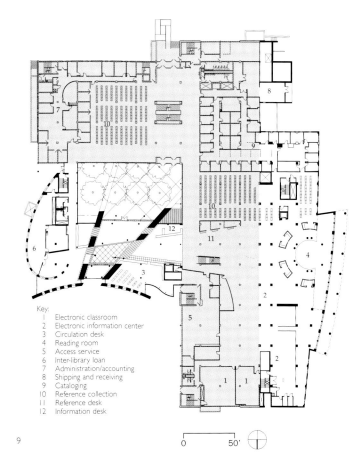

Key:
1   Electronic classroom
2   Electronic information center
3   Circulation desk
4   Reading room
5   Access service
6   Inter-library loan
7   Administration/accounting
8   Shipping and receiving
9   Cataloging
10 Reference collection
11 Reference desk
12 Information desk

9

0   50'

10

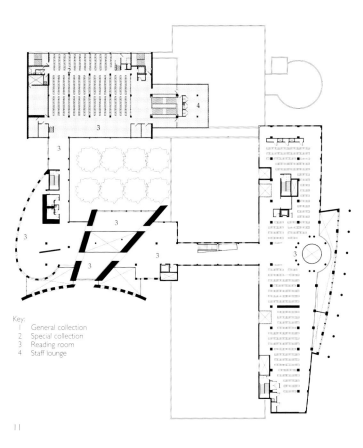

Key:
1 General collection
2 Special collection
3 Reading room
4 Staff lounge

11

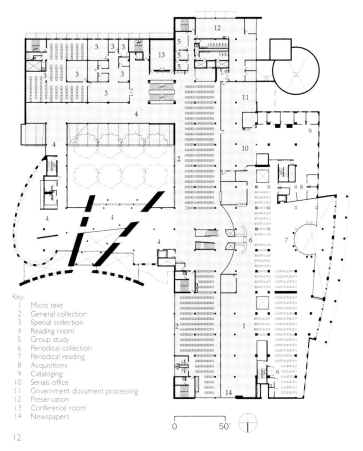

13

Key:
1   Micro text
2   General collection
3   Special collection
4   Reading room
5   Group study
6   Periodical collection
7   Periodical reading
8   Acquisitions
9   Cataloging
10 Serials office
11 Government document processing
12 Preservation
13 Conference room
14 Newspapers

0   50'

12

Kennewick Library
Buffalo Design

This library in Kennewick, Washington is the anchor of a new 20-acre municipal park created from a former fruit orchard. Beyond its immediate residential neighbors, the vast Columbia Basin landscape surrounds the park, punctuated by basalt outcroppings and distant views of the Cascade Mountains.

The client wanted a building that would feel at home in its expansive setting. It was to be appropriate to its physical environment, sheltering occupants from the perpetual, harsh south winds and strong sun, while also emphasizing the beauty and bright sunlight of the region. The library would also be an integrated element of the new park, with connections between the social and intellectual pursuits inside and the recreational activities outside.

The 32,000-square-foot building is planned around the metaphorical confluence of the Columbia, Yakima, and Snake Rivers, which are the circulation paths organizing the library's various collections. Expressed in colored aggregate concrete and studded with glass tiles, the 'rivers' begin outside in the park and entry plaza. They lead patrons the length of the building before finally passing back through the library walls and into community garden spaces beyond. Along the way are displays of art and local events, an information desk at the building's center, and a new book collection and reading lounge organized around a central fireplace. Study areas and lounges reach out into the park, framing views to northwestern vistas.

Strong, dynamic forms and materials are borrowed from the agricultural warehouses and processing plants that are a familiar sight in the area. Ordinary construction materials such as tilt-up concrete walls, metal roofs, and exposed steel structural elements are employed not only for economy but also to help connect the library, as a center of information and community, with the other elements of everyday life in the area. Colors are inspired by the basalt hills, the seasonally changing crops and desert grasses, and the rich reds and browns of the soil.

5

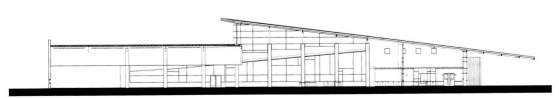

4

Paul Cummins Library

Steven Ehrlich Architects

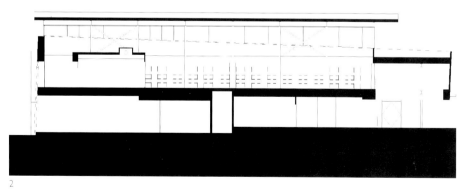

The heart of the Crossroads Middle and Secondary School in Santa Monica, California is a private alley that doubles as a parking lot and as a student-gathering courtyard. Set among a hodgepodge of converted warehouses and industrial structures, the new Paul Cummins Library is an 'offering' to the campus. As such, the two-story periodical reading room penetrates into the 'campus quad' (alley). Its location symbolizes the 12,000-square-foot library's greater importance in the school fabric and invites students in.

Approximately half of the new library's ground floor is dedicated to three classrooms that serve an adjacent math center. The remaining space fronts the alley and acts as the building's entry and meeting area, circulation department, and informal reading lounge. An open stair and mezzanine lookout beckon students to the second level, which houses the library proper.

Book stacks and administrative support facilities are positioned under flanking low roofs that serve reading and study areas. These are centrally located within a two-story volume vaulting toward the north-facing clerestory windows. The windows allow natural light during the day and help conserve energy.

The library is contained by a series of folded planes of exterior plaster rendered in blue, which descend in elevation from a peak at the rear elevation down to the pedestrian alley front. A steel canopy offers a shaded gathering place and leads into the double-height entry volume. Vibrant yellow exposed structural steel framing supports the structure and inclined wall.

1 At night, library becomes a beacon in the neighborhood

2 Section

opposite: Interior of reading areas

5

6

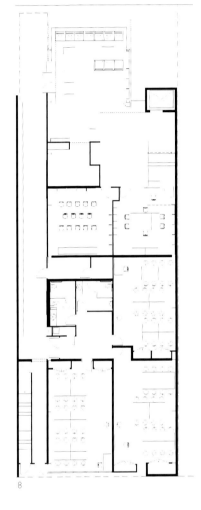

4 Library's street-side elevation

5 Light filters in from clerestory windows

6 Generous staircase connects upper and lower levels

7 Double-height space on upper level

8 Floor plan

9 Carrels are found near library's back wall

photography: Erhard Pfeiffer

Slusser Memorial Library

Line and Space

The Postal History Foundation is an institution devoted to education, research, and the advancement of publications in the field of philately. Located adjacent to the existing Foundation building in Tucson, Arizona, the Slusser Memorial Library provides a forum in which postal history is organized, preserved, and provided, placing a premium on flexibility and maintaining special areas for users and collections.

Before the building was designed, an extensive contextual analysis was performed, assessing many existing features of the historical neighborhood. This revealed a variety of surface textures and treatments consisting of stucco, exposed masonry, raised stone foundations, and concrete or stone windowsills and lintels.

The library's scale and material palette evokes a strong reference to its historical context; its construction, while not extravagant, places value on quality. Of primary importance is the achievement of a sense of unity with the surrounding neighborhood, as well as the creation of a low-maintenance and cost-effective structure. Concrete block, the primary building material, is clad with stucco to help the structure blend into the context. Natural stone veneer for the angled entry wall evokes a strong reference to the historic use of this material, enticing patrons from the existing postal facility to the interior of the new library. Openings and concrete projections provide an exciting visual dynamic, reinforcing the desired connection with the historical.

The library responds to different climatic zones, using appropriate technological and passive responses to mediate the harsh Tucson microclimate. Large roof overhangs shade the floor-to-ceiling windows of the reading room and provide a thermal and visual transition from the harsh exterior sun to the cooler, darker interior.

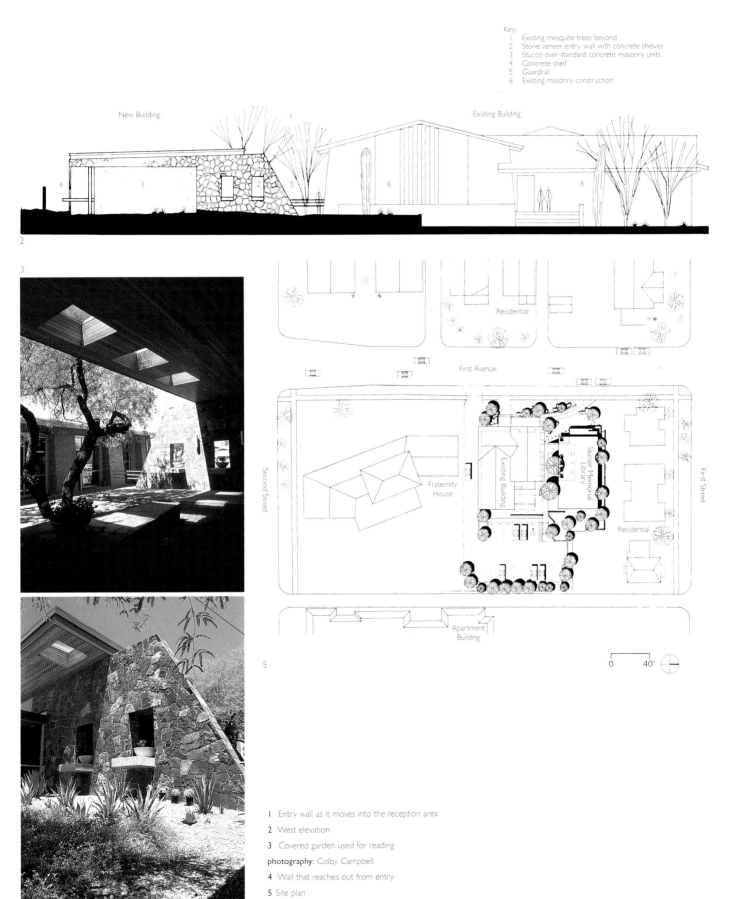

Key:
1 Existing mesquite trees beyond
2 Stone veneer entry wall with concrete shelves
3 Stucco over standard concrete masonry units
4 Concrete shelf
5 Guardrail
6 Existing masonry construction

New Building

Existing Building

4 3 2 5 1 6 6

2

3

First Avenue

Residential

Second Street

Fraternity House

Existing Building

Slusser Memorial Library

First Street

Residential

Apartment Building

0   40'

5

1 Entry wall as it moves into the reception area

2 West elevation

3 Covered garden used for reading

photography: Colby Campbell

4 Wall that reaches out from entry

5 Site plan

photography: Les Wallach, FAIA

4

6

6 Veneer stone captures desert colors
photography: Colby Campbell
7 Detail of plant stand in entry wall
photography: Les Wallach, FAIA
8 View from inside covered garden used for reading
9 Reception area with hovering ceiling
10 View toward entry
photography: Colby Campbell

Rauner Special Collections Library
Dartmouth College
Venturi, Scott Brown and Associates

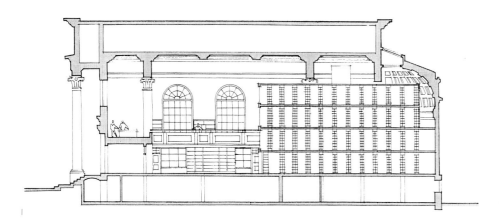

In 1901, Charles A. Rich designed Dartmouth's main auditorium building, which was supplanted in the 1960s by a separate performance facility, and thereafter sat underutilized on an important site facing the campus green. The design challenge was to transform the building into an accessible, functional, and visually evocative library with 30,000 linear feet of rare books and manuscripts housed in a secure and carefully controlled environment. The scope of the renovation also included a reading room, study, and seminar rooms, offices, and technical support spaces.

The solution preserves the monumental interior hall as the reading room, which accommodates 36 users and is surrounded by shelves of reference materials. As the original exterior walls of the building could not effectively provide thermal and moisture protection for the controlled collections space without substantial modifications, an aluminum and glass curtainwall enclosure was designed to create a transparent 'building within a building.' This glazed lantern of book stacks maintains temperature and humidity levels for the sensitive collection, protecting them in a vapor-tight conservation environment, while making them more visually accessible.

continued

3

1 Longitudinal section; special collections in Webster Hall
2 View from lobby into collections library
3 Reading areas on mezzanine level
4 Axial view of special collections library

4

Lighting reinforces the dialogue between the original building and the new. Old theatrical lighting was replaced with a fiber-optic system, similar in appearance to the original incandescent bulbs but more energy efficient and accessible from the attic above for relamping. Downlights recessed in the ceiling coffers provide ambient light and are supplemented by task lighting on study tables and bookshelves within the reading room. Inside the curtainwall enclosure, collections are washed with light to create a glow within the reading room and dramatically reinforce the importance of the collections.

The new special collections library is a dialogue between the original neoclassical and the new. The machine-like curtainwall is juxtaposed with gentle detailing on the walls, ceiling, and balcony front, while the millwork and curtainwall relate to the original building's variety of scales. Decorative plaster elements were restored to preserve a sense of the original interior while accommodating current needs.

5

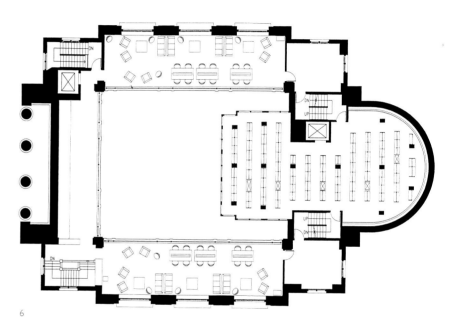

6

7

0   16'

8

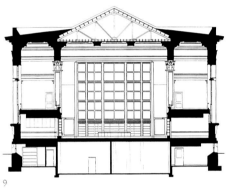

9

5 Detail of special collections curtainwall

6 Balcony level floor plan

7 First floor plan

8 View from reading room out to campus

9 Section

10 Variety of reading spaces are offered

photography: Matt Wargo

10

Issaquah Library
Bohlin Cywinski Jackson

This building in Issaquah, Washington is a 15,000-square-foot branch library that represents an expansion and modernization of library services for Issaquah in a more prominent and centralized location. The building is situated in the heart of the historic downtown core, on the corner of Front and Sunset streets. While future downtown planning calls for multistory urban structures, the library use dictated a single story. The cedar-sided structure resolved this apparent conflict by using an exaggerated building height coupled with the use of a trellis and canopies to maintain a humane scale at street level. These scale elements relate to the cornice height of the neighboring buildings and visually secure the library structure in its context.

Patrons approach the building's entry from the new parking structure, passing screens of greenery and artwork, and from Front Street past large multi-paned windows. This rhythm echoes the pattern of shop windows lining the street and offers protection through a large overhang and canopies. On the corner of the building is a large covered area, or agora, which serves as a sheltered gathering space and marks the library's entrance. Activity in the multipurpose room, adjacent to the agora, is visible from the streetscape. Doors open to the area outside to accommodate special events.

Entering the building from the agora, one passes through a wood-lined lobby and under a pair of tilted columns into the main space. Additional round columns gently taper, accentuating their height, as they rise to meet the wood-lined ceiling. Light filters in through the clerestory windows to highlight a delicate metal truss at the spine of the building and bathe the space in natural light.

continued

1 Concrete and canopies lend character
2 Children's area allows views of neighborhood
3 Exposed structure distinguishes interior
opposite: Lobby into building's reception area

5

6

7

5 View of roof structure at night

6 Wood canopy marks library entrance

7 Natural light floods interior

8 Trellis in front of parking garage

9 South elevation

10 Library commands its place on the streets' corner

11 Roof structure as it meets concrete column

12 Floor plan

photography: James Frederick Housel

8

Custom maple desks and bookcase ends carry the warmth of wood throughout the space. Trellises at the children's area and circulation desks mimic the exterior trellis. Stone petroglyphs in the floor and benches and a series of bronze ravens flow through the building. The artwork lines the entrance sequence from exterior to interior, drawing one into the building and echoing the sense of discovery inherent in the building's design.

9

10

11

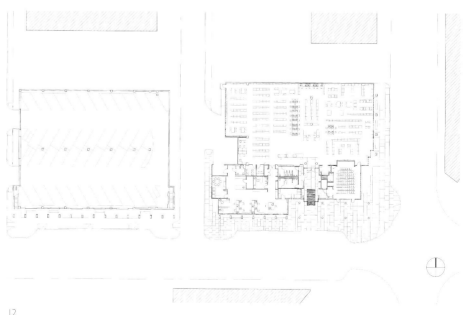

12

Boston Public Library Restoration and Renovation

Shepley Bulfinch Richardson and Abbott

1
2

This classical 1895 Charles McKim Building is the centerpiece of the Boston Public Library. As one of America's premier public libraries and one of Boston, Massachusetts' most prominent and frequently used public institutions, the National Historic Landmark building has remained fully operational throughout the life of the multi-phase project.

The primary objectives that guided the project were to preserve the historic fabric of the building; to conserve the artwork throughout the interior; to upgrade and expand the building's public services in an age of changing technologies; to encourage public use of the building, and to facilitate access to its extensive research collections.

The project presented the formidable task of restoring historically significant architectural spaces and their rich integral adornment of associated murals and sculptures. At the same time, all building spaces required extensive reorganization and adaptation for contemporary functional use. The project also included replacing all major M/E/P systems and enabling the installation of technology systems and infrastructure, while preserving the magnificent, historic interior.

In earlier phases, the original McKim Building main entry lobby and grand stair were restored to their original grandeur, including the conservation of fine art; the reopening of architecturally significant spaces that previously housed collections for public use, including provisions for a future tea room and exhibition space; and the reclaiming of the lower level—previously used for storage—for public access to government documents and a future maps department.

continued

3

4

The most recent work has involved the restoration of Bates Hall (main reading room), the exterior courtyard arcade, and the periodical and catalog departments. Also completed at this time was the northwest corridor, which connects the 19th-century architectural style of the McKim Building with the contemporary library annex designed by Philip Johnson. Future work will include further restoration of remaining historic rooms (Cheveres and Abbey Rooms and Sargent Gallery), additional fine art conservation, and the renovation of administrative offices.

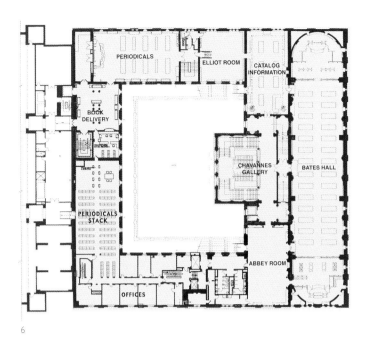

6

7

8

opposite: McKim Building's restored Bates Hall

6 Bates Hall floor plan

7 Basement lobby of McKim Building

8 Restored lobby space

photography: Richard Cheek

Lied Library
University of Nevada

Leo A Daly

This state-of-the-art library at the University of Nevada in Las Vegas houses a collection of two million books and scholastic resources, and 2500 reader stations for use by students and the public. It is conceived to be a friendly, flexible, and interactive learning environment that encourages collaborative study, idea interchange, and personal research.

The new 302,000-square-foot library serves as both a center of learning and as a beacon on campus, lighting the surrounding areas at night and providing collaborative study areas, as well as a lively environment in which students and the public may congregate. The public entry encourages interaction and social gathering, the meeting of friends, or participation in a festival or special campus event. Its architecture is a combination of rounded and angular forms, which provide shaded meeting places along its perimeter that give the vast structure an intimate scale. The result is a new library that represents the future—a dynamic blend of technology and design that is highly efficient, flexible, and welcoming.

The library harvests natural daylight to offset lighting and cooling costs while deflecting heat. The exterior skin includes low-e insulated glass, perforated aluminum sun louvers, and deflectors. Zinc alloy skin cladding on 'floating' vertical walls and the barrel-vaulted roof deflect the heat. Interior lighting is computer-friendly, indirect, and controlled to monitor changing daylight conditions.

continued

1 View of library from southeast

2 Library's north elevation

3 Information commons is a main interior space

3

4

5

The interior spaces, bathed in indirect natural light, are centered on a dramatic barrel-vaulted, five-story 'living room.' A glass-clad volume protrudes into the atrium space housing reading rooms. Reading carrels are stacked along the north wall offering natural light and great views of the skyline. An open sculptural stair, escalator, and elevators link all levels above ground, including the library administration suite, a thermally isolated special collection/archive department, reader stations distributed throughout the library collection, and an honors suite. A 100-seat, extended-hours study/coffee shop is located on the ground floor.

6

4 Conference room offers spacious views

5 Information commons is populated with computer terminals

6 Reading areas overlook information commons

7 Reading areas offer light and views

8 Study carrels are found throughout the library

9 Entry is protected by welcoming awnings

photography: Paul J. Brokering

7

8

9

Mary Baker Eddy Library
The First Church of Christ, Scientist

Ann Beha Architects

1

This new library contains the Mary Baker Eddy collections, housing 20,000 volumes, and spaces for exhibitions, conferences, and family programs. At 81,000 square feet, this is the largest library dedicated to an American woman, and it is designed to engage the public in her ideas about spirituality and transformation.

The library is housed in a neoclassical building in the Back Bay neighborhood of Boston, Massachusetts, formerly the home of the *Christian Science Monitor*. The design is a strong civic intervention along Massachusetts Avenue; a surrounding high wall penetrated, breached yet intact in some of its characteristic features: the pedimented arched gateway and rusticated corners at each end. By raising and redesigning the overgrown sunken garden, a new entry plaza is created—a respite from the noisy urban street.

The visitor is invited through this garden to discover an urban oasis with planting, trees, and benches. A waterfall terminates in a shallow crescent-shaped pool, and the granite wall is incised with a quote from Mary Baker Eddy. The pool reflects the new 16-foot-high glass and stainless-steel entrance pavilion, intersecting with the original limestone entry. This new glass wall mirrors its surroundings through its faceted surfaces and at night, it is an illuminated beacon. The new library entrance celebrates transparency and welcome.

continued

1 View through library's glass wall
photography: Brian Vanden Brink
2 Classical entry into Hall of Ideas
3 Library interior is rendered in light
  colors and dark woods
4 Courtyard buffers entrance
photography: Jonathan Hillyer/Esto

A restored reception area features a flight of steel and glass. The stair is also designed as a clear, contemporary intervention in the original building, extending the design vocabulary from outside to inside. The library occupies four floors, with two floors dedicated to exhibits, including the restored original Mapparium. At the reception area, the architects have installed an open glass and steel stair connecting arrival to the permanent exhibitions. The library's public collections and conference center are located in adjacent spaces on the third floor, designed in a simple, contemporary vocabulary of red birch and glass, with contemporary and traditional furnishings. The fourth floor is reserved as a scholar's study and research floor, with spaces for collections study, archives, and collections conservation.

5

6

7

8

9

5 Exterior of entrance as it faces courtyard

photography: Jonathan Hillyer/Esto

6 Detail of curved glass wall

photography: Brian Vanden Brink

7 Reception area with its contemporary staircase

8 Gate leads to courtyard oasis

9 View from reception lobby out to courtyard

10 Hallway features mosaic ceilings

photography: Jonathan Hillyer/Esto

10

Eltham Public Library

Gregory Burgess Architects

Eltham, Victoria, Australia has long had a sense of pride in being a community aware of both art and ecology. In the 1930s and 1940s artist and architect Justus Jorgenson built Monsalvat in Eltham as a vibrant center of artistic and cultural life, and Alistair Knox won historic council approval to build in earth in sympathy with the environment. Since then, Eltham has been proud of its identity as an artistically aware and environmentally active community. Its library is an expression of this community spirit, providing a popular and inspirational focus for a range of activities including community meeting and exhibition spaces, council art displays, and a small coffee shop.

The building sits on a combination of suspended concrete slabs, timber access decks, and earth berms carefully arranged to preserve the existing oak and peppercorn trees. Sympathetically set back from historic Shillinglaw Cottage, winding ramps and verandas lead visitors on a pleasurable journey to the center of the library.

1 Aerial view of library
2 Building's materials help it to blend with its surroundings
3 Information desk is flooded with light from above
4 Natural light washes wood ceilings

3

Within a concentric plan, the book stack areas extend radially from the center, allowing good sight lines from the central desk out to perimeter windows with landscape views and more casual reading areas. The clerestories reflect natural light off the curved timber ceilings, and ripple out from the center to divide the volume into a series of interconnecting planes, carefully balancing uplifting light and gentle grounded enclosure.

The design aims to inspire individuals, engaging the mind, the feelings, the senses, and the soul, balancing individual privacy with public sharing; knowledge with wisdom; active imagination with spatial calm; nature with culture; a still center with a dynamic periphery.

The building uses economical low-maintenance natural materials such as clay brick, mud brick, and radially sawn, plantation-grown timbers for external cladding and interior lining. Radially sawn timbers give better yields and more stable sections than conventionally milled timbers. Recycled timbers were used for veranda posts and openings revealed in the mud-brick walls. The main structural system incorporates natural timber poles in the ceremonial spaces.

4

5

6

7

5 Roof is scalloped to admit natural light

6 Organic forms and geometry are used throughout

7 Bird's-eye view of sinuous roof

8 Ground floor plan

9 North–south section

10 Undulating surfaces in ceiling of reading room

11 Information desk is a dominant element

photography: Trevor Mein

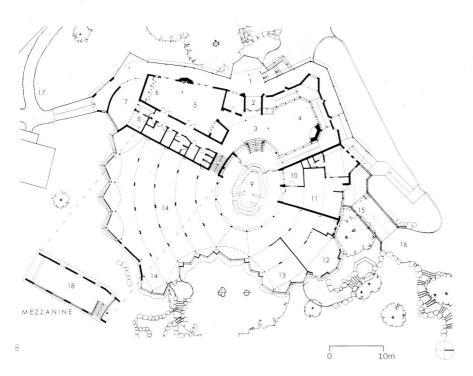

MEZZANINE

8

0   10m

Key:
1 Veranda
2 Entry
3 Foyer
4 Community display
5 Community multipurpose area
6 Children's toy library
7 Deck
8 Kitchen
9 Circulation desk
10 Librarian
11 Staff workroom
12 Children's area
13 Young adult area
14 Adult collection
15 Loading bay
16 Vehicle access
17 Footpath to Alistair Knox Park
18 Mezzanine level

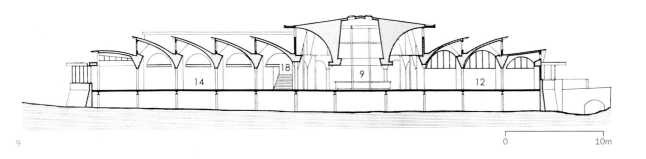

9

0   10m

10

11

Des Plaines Public Library
Lohan Caprile Goettsch Architects

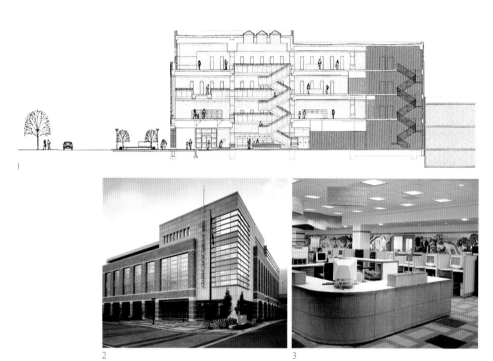

The new modern library in the City of Des Plaines, Illinois anchors the revitalization of the city's downtown area. The new library has nearly twice the space of its predecessor. Its timeless architectural aesthetic responds to the regional context and fulfills the community's desire for a civic landmark. A skylit atrium over the entry lobby provides patrons with a visible and psychological connection between the four levels of space. Service desks are placed in the same location on each floor and, together with a color-coordinated interior design and signage system, afford logical orientation for patrons. Open collections areas and modem data distribution offer a flexible facility. Warm-toned materials and numerous windows create a welcoming, comfortable environment.

Located directly across the street from the city's commuter train station, the library provides the community of Des Plaines with a civic landmark to be proud of, and is highly visible and accessible to citizens and visitors alike. As an anchor in the downtown area, the library and its landscaped plaza have already come to be the setting for community-wide events and ceremonies.

The new library has been a successful catalyst in the renaissance of the surrounding downtown. Since construction began, commercial and residential development in and around downtown has increased dramatically, and the community's pride in its city has also improved. In June 2000, then-Vice President Al Gore cited the redevelopment project as an example of the kind of 'new community development that's springing up in a lot of areas around community-based, affordable, and convenient mass transit,' which can revitalize a city.

1 Section

2 Glass-paned corner marks the entrance

photography: Les Boschke Photography

3 Information desk near entrance

4 Mobile in entry lobby is bright and colorful

photography: Hedrich-Blessing

5 Third floor plan

6 Second floor plan

7 First floor plan

8 At night the building is a prominent destination

photography: Les Boschke Photography

4

5

6

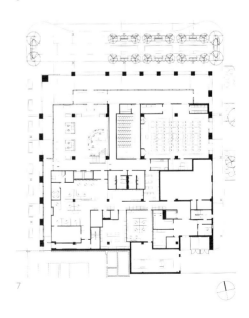

7

8

9

11

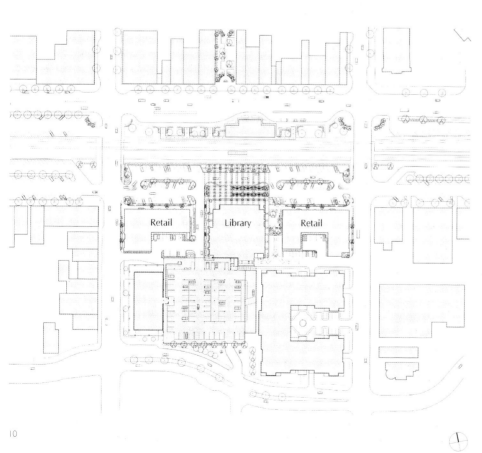

Retail   Library   Retail

10

12

13

9 Vibrant mural in children's area

photography: Les Boschke Photography

10 Site plan

11 Entry as it faces north

12 Reading area on third floor

13 Multistory lobby space

photography: Hedrich-Blessing

Sterling Memorial Library Restoration and Renovation Yale University

Shepley Bulfinch Richardson and Abbott

The renovations to this historic library at Yale University in New Haven, Connecticut are being completed in several phases, throughout which the library has been and will be permitted to remain in full operation.

Phase I focused on two major components. First was the renovation of the 17-level, self-supporting book stack tower to provide proper environmental conditions for the collection. This included new HVAC, electrical, telecommunications, fire protection, lighting, and elevator systems, as well as the replacement of existing windows and the restoration of the stone exterior. The second component was the restoration of the main reading room, periodicals reading room, exhibit corridor, memorabilia room, manuscripts and archives, and the American studies reading room.

Phase II involved the conversion of an existing open-air courtyard into a new multilevel music library. This adaptive reuse of space would help reduce energy loss in the existing building and minimize the 'footprint' of the overall complex. The music library effectively incorporates the former courtyard space and some adjacent floor space to form a 'building within a building.'

Contemporary, Gothic-inspired, arched trusses lift the new gently curved roof some 60 feet above the reference reading area, and are anchored to the library's existing steel-frame construction. Clerestories on all four sides of the space provide reflected indirect light onto the lightly colored ceiling and into the space below. Some of the major challenges of this project included building and installing the trusses; weaving new mechanical, electrical, and life safety systems into the existing building; and allowing Sterling Library to remain fully operational throughout construction.

2

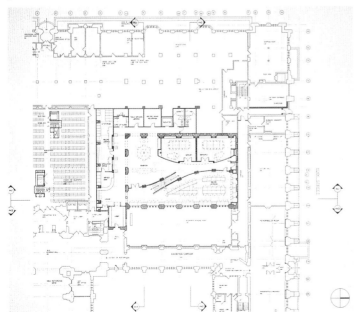

3

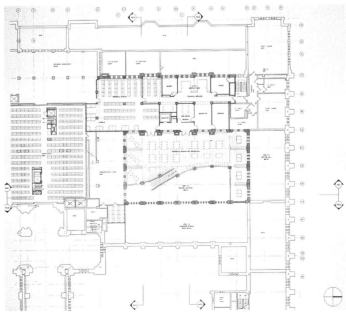

4

6

7

8

9

opposite: Arches in music library

6 Reading room in Sterling Library

7 Detail of light fixture in music library

8 Entrance to music library

9 Detail of trusses in music library

photography: Peter Aaron/Esto

South Jamaica Branch Library

Stein White Nelligan Architects

The new South Jamaica Branch Library in Queens, New York is the first building commissioned and completed under New York City's Department of Design and Construction Sustainable Design Program. Considered to be a civic anchor in a transitional neighborhood, the library addresses the three basic concepts of environmentally conscious design: the construction process should make minimum demands on the natural environment; the operation of the building should make minimal demands on the natural environment; the building should provide healthy and supportive conditions for all those who use it. The consideration of specific approaches to sustainable design also had to occur simultaneously with the resolution of library and community facility issues.

The most readily apparent 'green' aspects of the building fall into the second category: ecological building operation. The most significant of these relate to minimum energy consumption. The building uses an integrated combination of controlled daylighting, direct solar gain for heating, the exhaust of stratified air to reduce cooling loads, and careful placement of high and low thermal mass building materials to take advantage of passive heating and cooling. In its first year of operation, the building used less than 30 percent of the energy used by other comparably sized branches.

The approaches to daylighting and direct heat gain/controlled summer shading have created a dynamic interior environment with soft, diffused sunlight that is brighter and warmer in the winter and more subdued and sheltered in the summer. Applied finishes—both materials and coatings—are kept to a minimum. The basic building materials form the majority of the architectural surfaces.

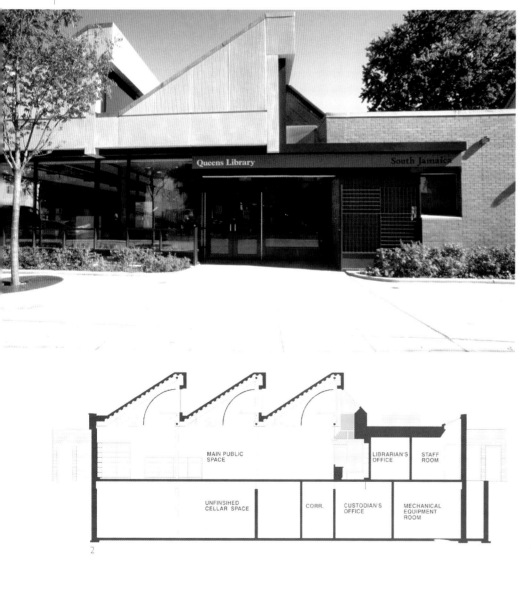

1 Color is judiciously used at entrance

2 Transverse section

3 Exposed mechanical equipment in library

4 Library entry is welcoming

The building is essentially at the property line on three sides and the street façade was designed to encourage and welcome visitors. The library's main room, defined by walls of brick and books, opens out through a transparent storefront onto a widened sidewalk. The composition consists of three primary components: the main room; the brick elements, which enclose it in plan; and the roof structure, which covers it and serves as the major interface between the exterior and interior environments.

3

4

5 Floor plan

6 View of central library space

7 Detail of entry gate

8 Natural light is filtered into interior

9 Detail of fenestration

10 Natural light floods central library

photography: courtesy Stein White Nelligan Architects

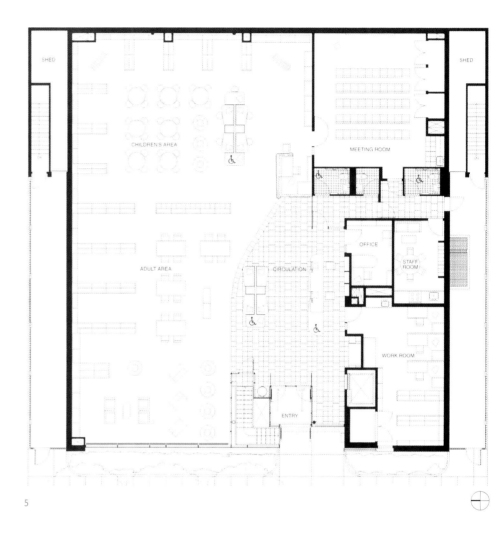

5

6

7

8

9

10

Biblioteca Latinoamericana

Steven Ehrlich Architects (Design Architect)
Garcia Teague Architecture + Interiors (Executive Architect)

Located one mile south of downtown San Jose, California, the Biblioteca Latinoamericana (including the Washington United Youth Center) anchors a 75,000-square-foot T-shaped site surrounded by commercial, educational, and residential uses. A shaded courtyard created by the space between the two buildings invites pedestrians through two different entrances via two shaded canopy/trellis pathways. This outdoor plaza becomes a neighborhood focal gathering place for everyday casual use, as well as special occasions such as fiestas and cultural events.

The buildings share a relationship of similar materials and forms that shelter an interior courtyard, accessible from both structures by roll-up glass doors. Each building is composed of tall masonry masses, formed from concrete block and brick that are held together by a lower, metal- and glass-clad element. The highest of these masses designate the central spaces for each with a gently vaulted metal roof and north-facing clerestory windows. Other high elements signify important spaces within both buildings.

The new library houses special collections of both Spanish and English literature that play a central role in the quality of community life. Biblioteca Latinoamericana is an important Spanish language resource in the region.

continued

1 Tower marks entry to youth center

2 Bright colors enliven exterior

3 Selection of materials is simple yet contextual

opposite: Front façade is articulated with light

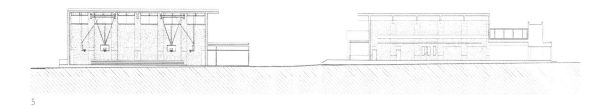

5

6

The symbolic public face of the project—a linear thickened mass that designates the entries for the library, parking, and courtyard beyond—creates a civic presence on the street. Stone, brick, and concrete block, which are woven together on both buildings in an abstracted Latin American-inspired pattern, make up the major material palette for the walls. A glass element emerges from the front façade and consists of floor-to-ceiling glass and stainless-steel panels. This element offers passersby a view into the library and patrons within a view to the city beyond. A program/community room where both library and youth center group programs can be planned, and community meetings occur, is positioned on the courtyard; roll-up glass doors in this room extend the space and allow meetings to spill outdoors.

8

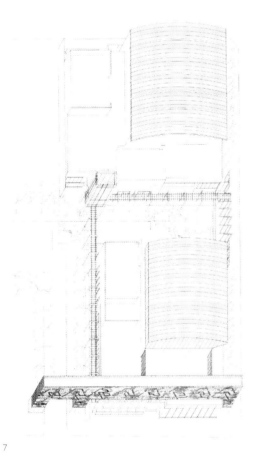

7

9

5 Elevations

6 Covered walkway that links buildings

7 Axonometric

8 Walkway connects library to 'young' building

9 Vehicular entry to inner sanctum of site

11

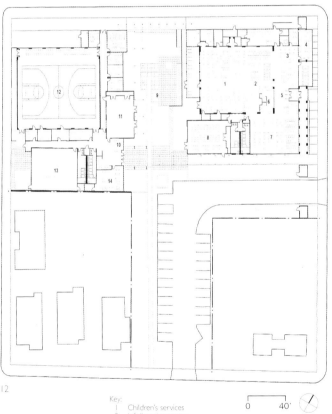

12

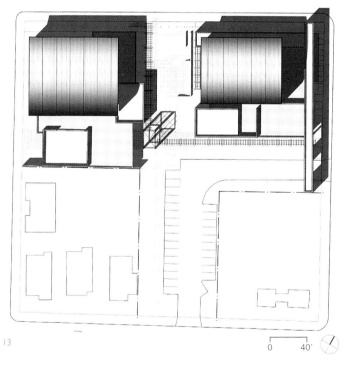

13

Key:
1 Children's services
2 Info/learning center
3 Young adult services
4 Magazines and newspapers
5 Entry
6 Service core
7 Adult stacks
8 Community room
9 Courtyard
10 Reception desk
11 Multipurpose
12 Gymnasium
13 Boxing/weight room
14 Games room

0   40'

opposite: Overarching ceiling gives library its great height

11 Library and youth center are behind street wall

12 Floor plans

13 Site plan

photography: Tom Bonner

Beaverton City Library

Thomas Hacker Architects

This library in Beaverton, Oregon is designed around a significant public room, constructed of an 'orchard' of graceful wooden columns arching upward into a wooden lattice of roof framing, which architecturally invokes Beaverton's nickname, the City of Trees. The library's setting is a new three-block park designed to accommodate a festive public market during warmer months.

The idea behind this building is deceptively simple: large central open spaces on ground and upper floors are circumscribed on three sides by more closed architectural elements. These protective masonry elements contain library support spaces and smaller public rooms. The fourth side of the roughly square plan is completely open to the south, becoming the main entrance facing the parks and the public market. There is a double-height entry portico, classical in its proportions but modern in its construction and character, and a generous lobby at ground level serving the library and the auditorium below. The second floor is open to the main reading room, like a large bay window, and holds special collections and study carrels that look out over the parks. This glazed concrete-framed porch performs the double function of filtering sunlight into the building's interior and representing the spacious public room within.

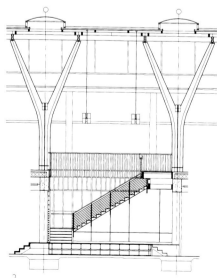

One enters the main reading room from another room below, centrally placed within the square plan and containing a double stair to the upper-floor reading room. The reading room is a peaceful courtyard oasis. The room is constructed of a series of delicate laminated-wood columns that gracefully splay up and out, blending seamlessly into an intricate lightweight supporting structure that floats above the space, much like a canopy of foliage in a forest. The richness of the natural wood ceiling suffuses the space with warmth that seems to glow against the gray Oregon sky outside. Although the size of the room is large, its scale is both intimate and comfortable.

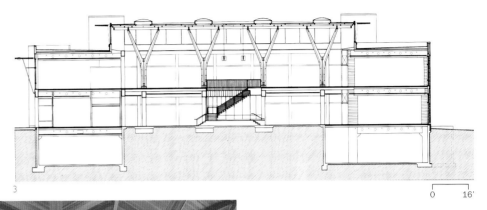

1 Library facing the park
2 Detail section
3 Cross section
4 Central stair is naturally lit from above
photography: Lara Swimmer

5 Second floor plan

6 Columns and trusses lend scale to interior

photography: John Hugel

7 First floor plan, park entry

opposite: Stair is rendered in elegantly detailed wood

photography: Stephen Miller

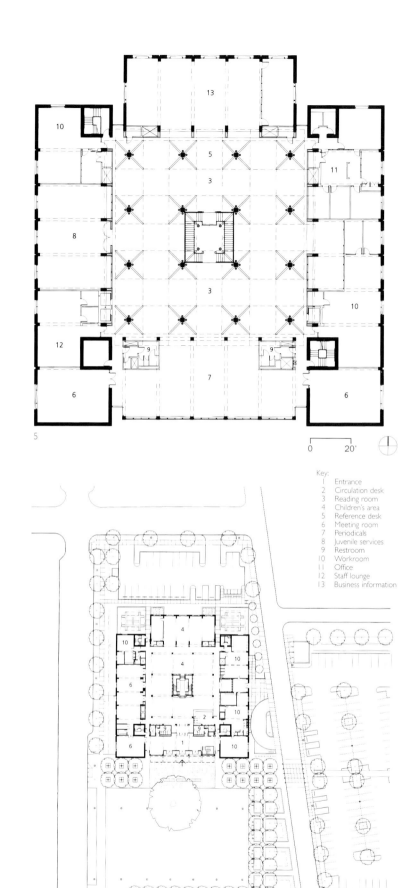

Key:
1 Entrance
2 Circulation desk
3 Reading room
4 Children's area
5 Reference desk
6 Meeting room
7 Periodicals
8 Juvenile services
9 Restroom
10 Workroom
11 Office
12 Staff lounge
13 Business information

9 Library entrance is directly off the street

photography: Lara Swimmer

10 Artwork and a sheltering airlock are found at entrance

photography: Stephen Miller

11 Airlock entrance is filled with sunlight

photography: John Hugel

12 Graceful wood arches distinguish interior

photography: Lara Swimmer

13 Orientation is achieved through central stair

photography: Stephen Miller

9

10

11

12

13

Waidner Library
Dickinson College
Perry Dean Rogers | Partners Architects

1   2

This new library is an addition to the Spahr Library, a 72,000-square-foot, three-story library built in the 1960s on the Dickinson College campus in Carlisle, Pennsylvania. The Waidner Library addition, 46,000 square feet in size, provides new stack and reader spaces, as well as a completely self-contained special collections reading and stack area. The addition links to the existing library on Spahr's west side with a glazed connection that clearly separates new from old. However, these glass-paned walls replicate Spahr's tripartite horizontal window division—a subtle, harmonic reference.

The addition also integrates the Spahr Library, a late-International Style building, into the older, Civil War era campus fabric by synthesizing contemporary forms and old materials. The new library utilizes the same ashlar limestone used throughout the original campus, which was brought from the original quarry. A wood window system reflects both the windows of the older campus buildings and the monumental window organization of the Spahr.

continued

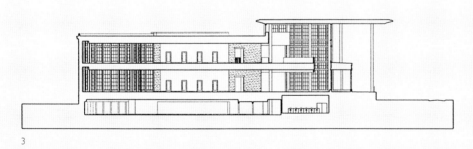

3

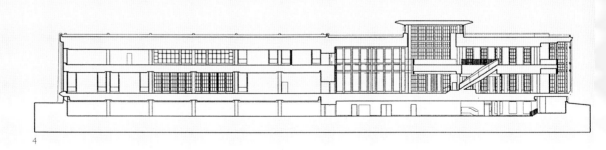

4

9   10

The interiors integrate the two buildings by placing the circulation desk in the two-story, linking space. 'The nest,' a curvilinear space over the circulation desk, is an intimate student lounge with a fireplace. The addition has an oval reading area overlooking Dickinson Walk, a pedestrian parkway bordering the northern edge of the library. A formal entry plaza, stair, and canopy face the street. The Waidner Library addition along with the existing Spahr building has wiring for power and dataports at every study carrel, reading room, and office. The library complex links to on-line services throughout the college.

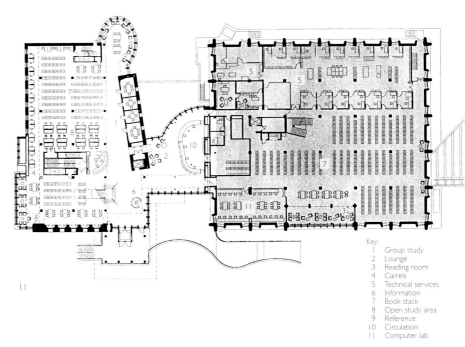

11

Key:
1 Group study
2 Lounge
3 Reading room
4 Carrels
5 Technical services
6 Information
7 Book stack
8 Open study area
9 Reference
10 Circulation
11 Computer lab

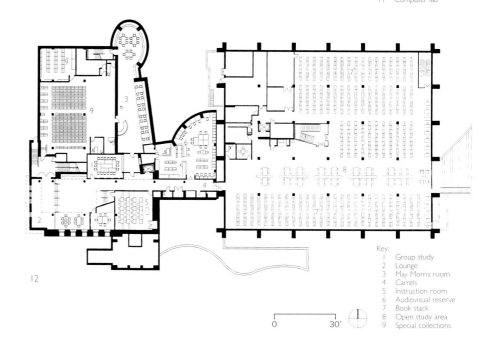

12

Key:
1 Group study
2 Lounge
3 May Morris room
4 Carrels
5 Instruction room
6 Audiovisual reserve
7 Book stack
8 Open study area
9 Special collections

0   30'

9 Light wood is used throughout interior

10 Rare book display near reading areas

11 Entry level floor plan

12 Lower level floor plan

13 Portico at night is a welcoming beacon on campus

14 Windows admit generous light and views

15 Reading area accentuates views of campus

16 Carrels offer more private study areas

photography: Richard Mandelkorn

Woodstock Library

Thomas Hacker Architects

At the intersection of two streets, one commercial and one residential, this small public library is conceived as a neighborhood living room. Under an enveloping roof, a single large room—almost an extension of the street—provides a place for reading, working, and meeting. The room's floor is level with the sidewalk, without the formal base or plinth that often lifts a public edifice, symbolically and literally, above the life of the city. This reinforces the library's role as a constituent of this Portland, Oregon community's daily life.

The building is designed to be a place that is both everyday and remarkable. Inside, the main room skillfully blends the dignity of a temple with the scale and comfort of a pavilion. Six pairs of graceful steel cruciform columns support a single flat roof plane, defining the main space of the room. The roof structure is an individual large canopy of gridded steel beams and decking that extends out past the columns, cantilevering over clerestory windows below, for shade and protection, as natural light filters into the room from all four sides.

At the street edge, the building skin (a curtainwall with alternating stainless-steel and aluminum panels) reveals the structure of the room to the street. The artwork and passages of literature etched into the metal panels are themselves in the grand tradition of urban public libraries and add to the library's civic quality.

Every piece of the building is meticulously detailed and sized to create a sense of loft inside the room and yet not overpower the residential scale of the surrounding neighborhood. The elements of construction recreate the scale of a classical building without the use of historicist references. Such attention to detail, scale, and proportion allows this building, constructed almost entirely of steel, to have a sense of comfort and ease normally only achieved with more traditional materials.

2

1 Main entrance to library

2 Children's area is light and open

3 Cross section

4 North elevation

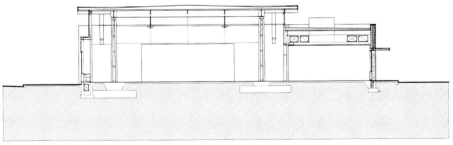

3

4

0   10'

5

6

7

5 North elevation with etched metal panels

6 Detail of etched metal panel

7 Interior is rendered in white

8 Exterior is expressive of construction system

9 First floor plan

10 West elevation

photography: Timothy Hursley

8

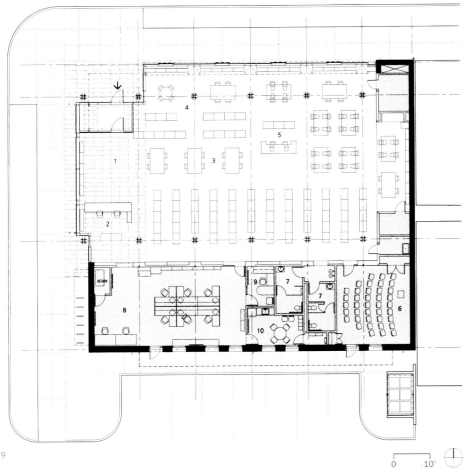

Key:
1 Entrance
2 Circulation desk
3 Reading room
4 Children's area
5 Reference desk
6 Meeting room
7 Restroom
8 Workroom
9 Office
10 Staff lounge

9

0   10'

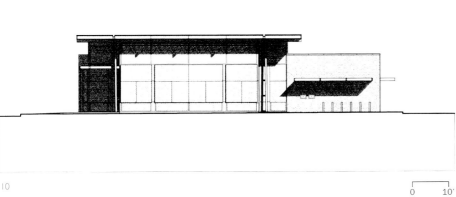

10

0   10'

Johnson County/Blue Valley Library

Gould Evans

The goal of this design was to create an 'enlightened,' 25,000-square-foot library for Overland Park, Kansas. It includes such patron-friendly features as a full-service drive-up window, drive-up book return, beverage café, public meeting room, and art gallery.

The library is the second component of a planned community center development in an edge city south of Kansas City. The district the library serves is populated, largely, by affluent professionals who have young children and homes built within the last decade. In addition to the library, the community development will include an elementary school, community center, pool structure, walking trails, and park. Facilities will share parking to minimize the paved surface.

Inside the library, the art gallery, café, performance courtyard, and other features augment the collection of 20,000 books, technology, and other resources. Some patrons, however, utilize the library services from the car through extensive drive-up services.

continued

Key:
1 Entry
2 Circulation
3 Art gallery
4 Reading area
5 Youth services
6 Audiovisual
7 Adult services
8 Meeting room
9 Café
10 Service window
11 Staff
12 Mechanical
13 Courtyard

1 View of library from south

2 Floor plan

opposite: View of library from courtyard

0   40'

The program demanded interaction between patrons in vehicles and the building itself, and this was achieved through a design concept that involves the rotation of space and planes around a centrally focused courtyard. The semicircular plan layers volumes of space; the negative space between the general public library collections and the staff areas maintains all of the public features of the program. This space is defined by the surrounding programmatic edges and glass walls at each end. Continuous clerestory glazing allows this public space to remain as open and part of the changing day as possible.

The courtyard, which can been seen in any of the public areas of the library, features a rock garden, seating boulders, a butterfly garden, xeriscape plantings, coniferous and deciduous trees, and a sculptural sun filter of perforated metal. The sun filter's plan and elevation are configured completely by the path of the sun for the winter and summer solstices. By allowing the filter to be constructed of perforated metals, it does not block the view from inside the library; instead, it colors it.

4 Canopy is rendered in enamel panels
5 Curved wall with view towards reading area
6 Interior is welcoming and light-filled
7 Corner detail near library entry
8 Canopy announces entry of library

photography: Mike Sinclair

7

8

Library Expansion and Addition
Oakton Community College

Ross Barney + Jankowski Architects

The library of Oakton Community College in Des Plaines, Illinois was constructed in 1978 as part of the original campus. Since then, the campus has nearly doubled in size, yet the 19,000-square-foot library remained largely unchanged. The expansion and renovation project addresses lack of space, campus identity, functional interaction, and the ability to adapt to changing technology. The expanded facility includes library functions, instructional support and lifelong learning services and addresses changing technology as an instructional tool and information source by providing flexibility for current and future needs.

Located at the entrance to the campus, the library is the hub of Oakton Community College. The addition provides a needed identity for the library. Views were improved to the heavily wooded site, and opportunities for natural lighting in public areas were optimized.

The expanded building is three levels and approximately 30,000 square feet. All infrastructure systems, electrical, mechanical, and data systems were renovated. The library provides an oasis for study and research in this commuter college. As it faces south, the library displays a new identity in its curved staircase structure, which bow out from the building, wrapped in a glass and metal envelope. The staircase provides vertical circulation between all three levels, and becomes an important design element and orientation device in the new building. Inside, ceiling cove lighting is used to guide students on their path through the library. Carrel areas are located mostly along the building's exterior walls, and take advantage of generous natural lighting, along with views out over the campus.

1 Open stairs connect all three levels of library

2 Staircase becomes a beacon at night

3 Circulation desk starts visitors on path through library

4 Site plan

5 Library wing from southeast

3

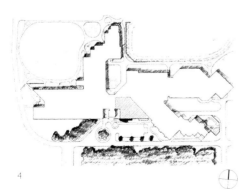

4

5

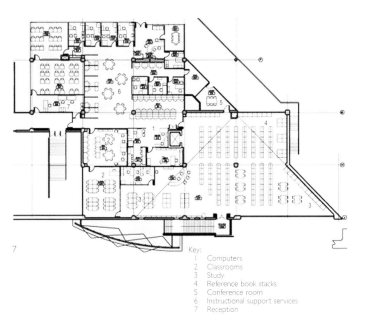

7

Key:
1 Computers
2 Classrooms
3 Study
4 Reference book stacks
5 Conference room
6 Instructional support services
7 Reception

10

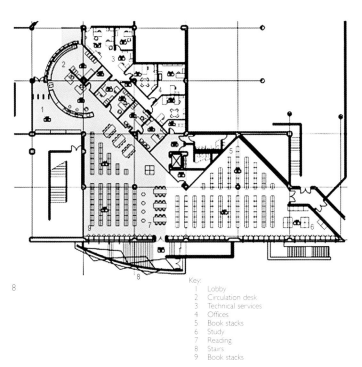

8

Key:
1 Lobby
2 Circulation desk
3 Technical services
4 Offices
5 Book stacks
6 Study
7 Reading
8 Stairs
9 Book stacks

11

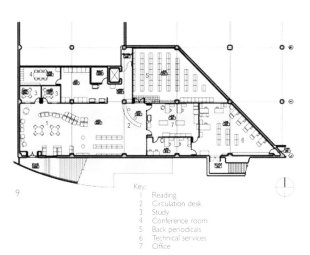

9

Key:
1 Reading
2 Circulation desk
3 Study
4 Conference room
5 Back periodicals
6 Technical services
7 Office

opposite: Light-filled, colorful staircase is a major space in the library

7 Second floor plan

8 First floor plan

9 Lower level floor plan

10 Carrel reading areas are enlivened with fabric structures

11 Circulation desk near entry

12

13

14

15

16

12 Library in its larger campus context

13 Ceiling recessed lighting helps in way-finding

14 South wall of building containing library

15 Staircase features light wood wall and views

16 Staircase emerges from library's south wall

photography: Steve Hall/Hedrich-Blessing

Mesquite Branch Public Library

Richärd & Bauer Architecture

1

This 18,000-square-foot project nearly doubled a busy branch library for the City of Phoenix, Arizona. The new program includes an expanded collection, new entry, meeting room and upgraded restrooms. Extensive renovation of the existing 10,500-square-foot structure includes expanded children's areas, a storytelling room, homework center and staff work areas.

The existing building's massive roof beams, simple folded wall planes, and the use of materials in their natural state serve as a strong foundation for the new work. All of these elements find expression within and outside the new library. An arc of vertical steel staves directs the path of the visitors to the new entry and unifies the new and old façades.

Extrusion of the main roof form captures the expanded adult collections area to the west of the existing building. The form slides across the existing building, exposing and contrasting the skeletal nature of the existing roof with the smooth scabbard of the expansion. Open steel trusses recall the rhythm and form of the massive concrete beams while creating a light and airy volume.

Natural gavalume, concrete, and glass are used to blend with the existing vocabulary. Mechanical systems thread their way through the interior and become an important design element. Light is brought in from high clerestories on the southern edge of the reading room, recalling the system used in the existing building. A mesquite tree-shaded court at the west end of the reading room provides patrons with an extended lounge area, light, and views.

1 Front elevation uses a combination of opaque and
transparent materials

2 Floor plan

3 Arc leads to entrance

4 Mechanical equipment becomes a design element in interior

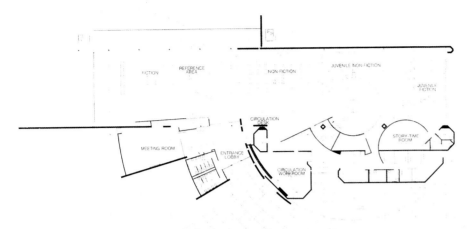

FICTION
REFERENCE AREA
NON-FICTION
JUVENILE NON-FICTION
JUVENILE FICTION

CIRCULATION DESK

MEETING ROOM
ENTRANCE LOBBY
CIRCULATION WORKROOM
STORY-TIME ROOM

0   32'

2

3

4

5

5 Exposed roof structure distinguishes library interior

6 Color is used judiciously in interior

7 View of entrance, with reading areas beyond

photography: Sally Schoolmaster

6

7

San Francisco Main Library

Pei Cobb Freed & Partners

1

This public library completes San Francisco's Civic Center, one of the few executed examples of the City Beautiful Movement of the early 1900s in America. To achieve this goal the library echoes the massing, materials, and formal development of neighboring institutions, simultaneously using the library's full-block site to forge a vital link between the 'contemporary city' and the Civic Center—a bridge between the people of San Francisco and the institutions that serve them. Underlying the design is a strategy of urban connection; the library is both a destination and a link that permits one to pass into and through the building, weaving the city to the Civic Center and the library to both.

Like its older counterpart across the street, the new library gestures formally with an L-shaped bar that offers two symmetrical façades complementary to the Civic Center. The library's two other façades make a more contemporary response to the commercial district.

Internally, the library is organized around two major spaces: a great open staircase that moves through the building, displaying its activities, and a five-story skylit open space, 60 feet in diameter, that connects the library's various parts. In both cases, the intention has been to bring natural light inside the 381,000-square-foot building.

On its lower level, the library houses meeting rooms and an auditorium that the public can use when the library proper is not open. Other amenities include literacy programs, services for the deaf and blind, and special programs for children. There are, in addition, exhibition spaces, a café and a bookstore, a small roof garden, and a special reading room visible from all areas of the building.

2

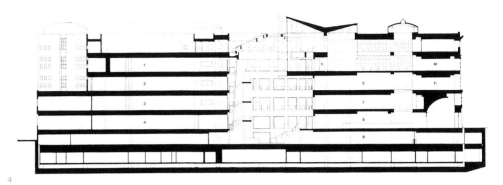

1 From northeast, library commands its site

2 Library from southeast, with view toward entry

3 View of library in its urban context

photography: Timothy Hursley

4 Section

5 Reading areas have the benefit of ample natural light

photography: Richard Barnes

6

7

8

6 View of main entry from lower level

7 Axial view of west elevation

photography: Jane Lidz

8 Overview of light-filled circulation area

photography: Timothy Hursley

9 Detail of east façade, with wing above

photography: Jane Lidz

10 Detail of west façade, with classically inspired elements

photography: Timothy Hursley

9

10

Lee B. Philmon Branch Library

Mack Scogin Merrill Elam Architects

Key:
1   Entry
2   Circulation desk
3   Computer catalogs
4   Reference/information
    desk
5   Periodicals/
    new books
6   Reference collection
7   Reading
8   Adult collection
9   Children's
    collection
10 Children's desk
11 Storage/kitchenette
12 Public meeting room
13 Public restrooms
14 Circulation
    work area
15 Manager's office
16 Mechanical/electrical
17 Staff lounge
18 Staff lockers
    and restrooms
19 Storage/workroom
20 Book return

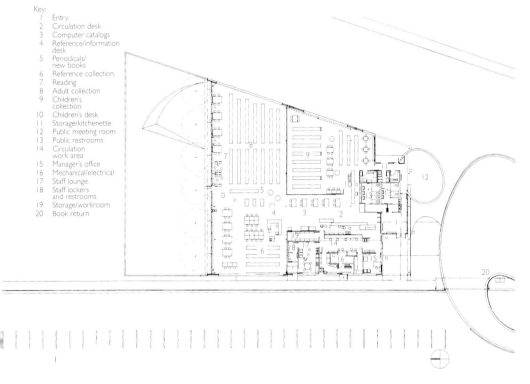

Within earshot of the Atlanta airport, in Riverdale, Georgia, this 12,000-square-foot library sits on a triangular-shaped leftover site wedged between properties slated for development. Corralled by sprawling suburbia, the little library asserts itself with quietude within this rapidly changing landscape. Unlike the nearby Wal-Mart or the neighboring metal shed that houses the Living Waters Assembly of God, which announces itself with bold signage and clarifies its functions with familiar forms, the library is a mysterious brushstroke against a background of predictability. Its curiosity becomes its invitation to visit.

Inside, along with computers and books, is an oasis of variegated space and light. Giant pennant patterns of glazing filter the daylight and allow it to bathe the interior. These tapered geometries of the façade glazing mirror the slope of ordinary, wallboard-clad roof trusses inside. The trusses, which give shape to the ceiling, are installed with alternating slopes to provide an undulating play of space, and to bounce light and disperse sound. Skylights on top of each column further encourage the dappling of daylight.

continued

2

3

4

1 Floor plan

2 Exterior expresses bold geometry

3 Interior ceilings are tent-like

4 Courtyard on building's north side

Most of the library's functions, adult stacks, children's collections, casual reading and study tables, public computers, reference area, circulation, and staff lounge, share space under the expansive trellis-like ceiling. The barrel-shaped public meeting room is found to the south and the outdoor reading garden to the north. These two exceptions appear as solid masses outside the building. Inside they are habitable discoveries and moments of repose.

At the north end of the library, the reading tables and reference area look out onto the walled garden. Throughout the day, sunlight washes the slightly inclined ground plane, sending soft reflected light into the interior. The garden and its immature plantings are a buffer zone against the eventual but inevitable convenience store planned for the adjacent site to the north.

At the south and entrance façade, the site rolls gently downward to the now-realized parkway. The library sits at the crown of this hill, giving the small building a greater-than-actual presence and making it highly visible from the parkway.

5

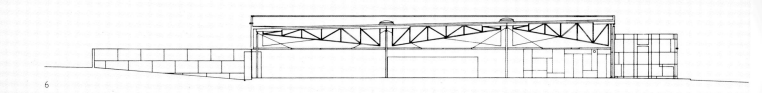

6

7

8

9

10

11

9 Entry with its gesticulating elements

10 View of building from east

11 Low wall creates protected courtyard

12 North wall contains reading areas and views of courtyard

photography: Timothy Hursley

12

University of the Sunshine Coast Library

Bligh Voller Nield Architects
John Mainwaring Architects (Associate Architects)

Commissioned to be the central structure on the emerging campus of Queensland's new Sunshine Coast University in Sippy Downs, this project rejects the tradition of libraries as internalized buildings, and opens up the interior to relate to the surrounding plain and sunny skies. Reading areas are located on the top floor where natural light is maximized. The circulation desk forms the focus of the middle level, and an art gallery occupies the ground floor.

The architectural proposition responds to its 'iconic' position, its microclimate, and to the language of inflected shading in southeast Queensland. It is an architecture that speaks of modern learning with the devices of informality, transparency, complexity, and lightness. The celebratory space is external—a great Queensland 'veranda'—which sets up the campus axis as a vista and establishes the library as a sociable, flexible focus of student culture.

The building pulls itself up above the landscape, riding on pilotis to command its surroundings. The canted roofs open the building up as a 'flying' structure, and to flood the upper levels with natural light. Different angles among the roof planes suggest movement along the building's profile. Natural materials on the exterior blend the building into its surroundings.

Meeting spaces, support spaces, and reception areas are found on the ground floor. Upper stories are devoted to stack spaces, with tables and reader space dedicated along its glassy periphery.

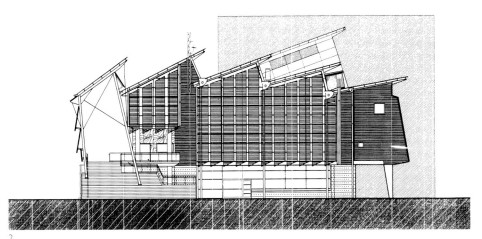

1 Library reveals its transparent nature

2 Elevation

3 Detail of building's canopied opening

4 Library rises above the landscape

5 Library's variegated elevation

photography: Anthony Browell

3

4

5

Maywood Library
Addition and Renovation

Ross Barney + Jankowski Architects

Maywood, Illinois is an inner-ring Chicago suburb. Economic depression and gang crime have plagued the town in recent years. The Maywood Library Board's decision to undertake a major expansion to the town's 7000-square-foot, 1908 Carnegie Library was a courageous attempt to create a catalyst for the revitalization of the community. After a true grassroots campaign that included enlisting every church in Maywood, the library became one of the very few library districts to pass a building referendum in Illinois.

The design of the addition reflects the Board's hopeful and progressive outlook while maintaining the integrity of the historic Carnegie. A cylindrical lobby and stair carefully separate the much larger addition (30,000 square feet) from the original building. A masonry wall detailed to recall the physical presence of the Carnegie forms the façade of the addition. Behind this screen is a simple and elemental interior that clearly distinguishes the addition from the older building.

The biggest surprise comes in the entry lobby, a circular space that soars three stories. This space, paneled in light wood, is distinguished by a staircase that hugs its walls and provides vertical circulation throughout the library. Accessed from the cylindrical circulation core, the new library spaces stretch to the east as one large room on each floor. Support spaces and special function rooms are found on the addition's north side, while the south wall is punctured with windows to admit natural light.

Furniture designed by the architect reflects the clean simple design. Reading tables, computer stands, and end panels on the shelving are made of plywood. The children's furniture is of similar construction and detail, but finished in multiple colors. In the children's library, awning materials are used to create a childlike scale and atmosphere.

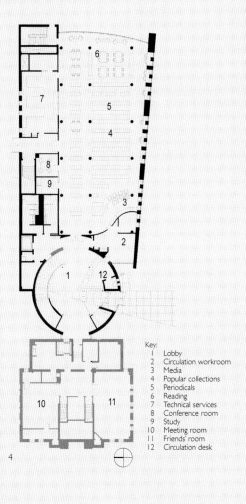

1 View of library entrance as it faces street

2 Entry is found through round element between the two buildings

3 View through first floor circulation area

4 First floor plan

Key:
1   Lobby
2   Circulation workroom
3   Media
4   Popular collections
5   Periodicals
6   Reading
7   Technical services
8   Conference room
9   Study
10 Meeting room
11 Friends' room
12 Circulation desk

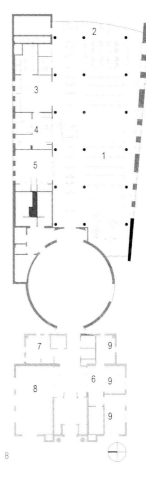

opposite: View of top of circular lobby space

6 Colors and shapes are used in children's area

7 Saucer-like light fixture in storytelling room

8 Second floor plan

9 Third floor plan

10 Stairway in circular lobby

11 Stacks on third floor under vaulted roof

12 Form of addition is distinguished by its
barrel-vaulted roof

photography: Steve Hall/Hedrich-Blessing

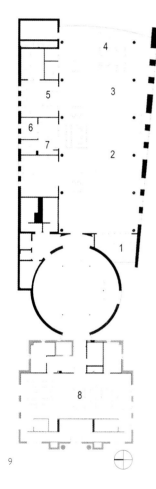

9

Key:
1 Quiet study
2 Adult services
3 Reference
4 Reading
5 Computers
6 Office
7 Workroom
8 Meeting room

10

Robertson Branch Library

Steven Ehrlich Architects

On busy Robertson Boulevard in Los Angeles, California, a civic building must compete for attention with its strip mix of traffic, billboards, and commercial buildings. The Robertson Branch library, with its pre-weathered, copper-clad 'ship's hull' protruding over the sidewalk, boldly yet gracefully announces its presence on the street.

The hull pierces the library's rectangular framework like a Yankee clipper bisecting a modernist block. The gracefully curved volume is energized by being slightly skewed on all three axes, heightening the counterpoint to the floor plan and elevation grids. The long axis is not perpendicular to the street, but points toward downtown and the main library, symbolically connecting the branch with the greater metropolis.

The 11,000-square-foot library squeezes onto a small site and concedes approximately three-quarters of the ground level to parking space. Only a multipurpose community room and administrative spaces are housed on the ground level, along with a stairway inside the vessel, which draws patrons upward. The reading room, circulation and reference desks, and public spaces are all on the second level.

In the main reading room, sloping clerestory windows, round skylights, and a peek-a-boo portal window pour natural light into the area where patrons browse or access the library's computers. The green vessel, which makes its presence known on the street, can be viewed throughout the building. It becomes a container of sunlight, which constantly shifts within this chamber throughout the day, and helps to track the passage of time. It also assists in orienting the visitor.

1 Dramatic lighting enhances library's presence
2 Library's strong street presence
3 View into circulation and stack area
opposite: Inside the green vessel, filled with light

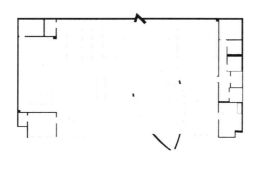

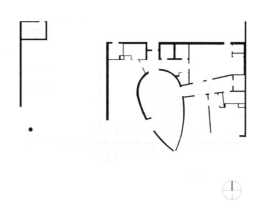

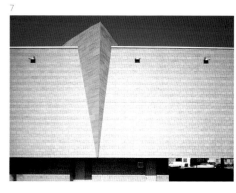

7

8

9

photography: Tom Bonner

10

11

Ron E. Lewis Library
Lamar State College

Leo A Daly

Over the years, the Lamar State College campus in Orange, Texas has developed from the acquisition of properties in the downtown area, which did not afford the sense of a traditional 'campus' layout of open spaces, quadrangles, and vistas between campus landmarks. The client's charge to the master plan design team was to develop a collaborative process involving many in the college community, which, in turn, would lead to a new image for the 12-acre campus while providing support of the academic mission. The plan consolidates the campus into a four-block pedestrian zone by closing two through-streets and developing a system of walkways and defined open spaces, which lends it a sense of a traditional campus.

The first phase of the plan included site development and landscaping that defines the central campus zone, a new central energy plant, expanded classroom facilities and a new 47,000-square-foot main library and administration building, the Ron E. Lewis Library.

The new library/administration building anchors the center of the campus adjacent to a new 'campus green.' Covered arcades border the campus green, providing pedestrian connections to key buildings on campus. The three-story brick structure suggests the tradition of masonry construction in this region. The building houses library and media center functions on the first two floors and administration and student services on the top floor. The library provides a new academic image for the campus while maintaining compatibility with the existing context of brick buildings in the town's central district.

1 Main entry to library

2 Front elevation includes a loggia as it faces the campus

3 Circulation desk near library entrance

2

3

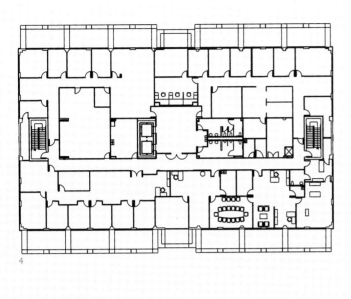

4

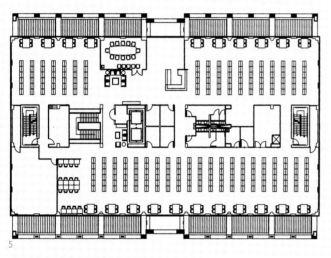

5

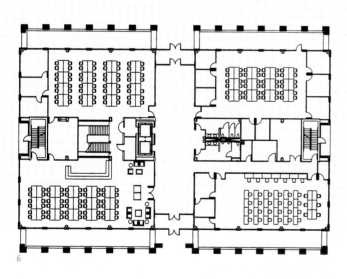

6

7

4 Third floor plan

5 Second floor plan

6 Ground floor plan

7 Library's spacious lobby

photography: Michael Wilson

Auburn Library
Olson Sundberg Kundig Allen Architects

The 15,000-square-foot Auburn Library in Auburn, Washington is designed to address the two divergent worlds that it borders. Sited on the edge of the suburban Les Gove Park, the library faces Auburn Way, a very busy highway. In response to the highway, the building forms a strong street presence, capable of calling attention to itself amidst the riot of color and signage typical of suburban thoroughfares. At the same time, the building softly modulates to meet the park that borders its opposite side.

With a roof shape reminiscent of an open book, the building is composed of two primary spatial areas, a large column-free collections area, and community resource and support areas, separated by a central spine. The spine contains the mechanical facilities and acts as a transition space between the two components of the building. The covered entry walkway takes its inspiration from the covered railroad platforms once common to Auburn, a prominent railway hub through the early 1900s.

Inside, the library has traditional stacks to hold over 100,000 books, as well as 50 computer stations. Particular attention was given to daylighting and electric lighting in the building. The primary lighting source for the collections area (80 percent of all supplemental lighting) is reflected light that bounces off the ceiling, reducing glare on computer screens, and creating a more pleasing reading environment.

The exterior is of two basic materials: brick and zinc. Brick suggests the importance of this civic structure and its durability, while zinc panels are used as a visual counterpoint. On the roof, the zinc is kept thin at the building's edges as reference to the pages of a book. The details of the building are, in large part, mathematically inspired. The Golden Section and the Fibonacci sequence were used to determine building heights, window divisions, and other aspects to add a layer of refinement to the building, as well as an educational side note.

0   80'

1 Detail of southeast exterior corner shows main collections room at dusk

2 Site plan

3 General view of library from southeast

4 Main circulation area, looking toward information desk

5 Floor plan
6 General view of library with exposed structure
  in ceiling
7 View from southwest, showing entry to library
8 Detail of exterior view of entry

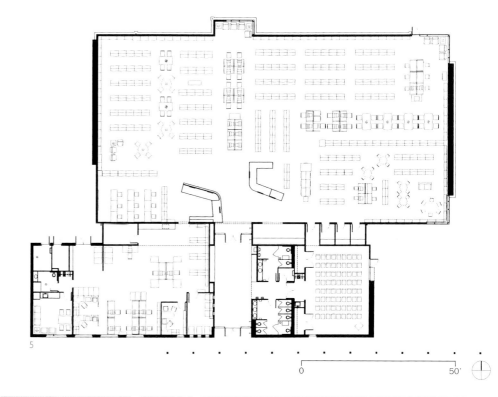

5

0   50'

6

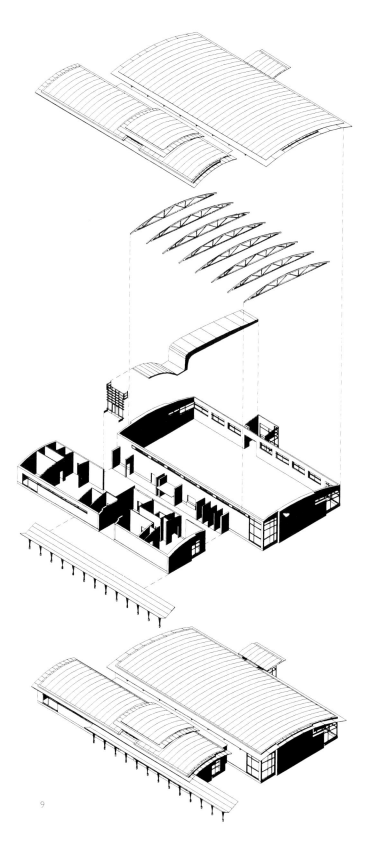

9 Exploded axonometric

10 View west through circulation area

11 Children's section has views from large window

12 Reflected light plays major role in circulation area

photography: Eduardo Calderon

Hyde Park Branch Library
Schwartz/Silver Architects

One of the branches of the public library system of Boston, Massachusetts, the original Hyde Park Library was built in 1899 in the classical revival style. It remained essentially unchanged until an expansion, restoration, and renovation program was undertaken that more than doubles the size of the facility to over 28,000 square feet.

The challenge was how to enhance the character and integrity of the original historic building, while at the same time making it a functional part of a larger modern library. The original library was designed to be aloof and impressive, while the new library was to be open and inviting. Located in a residential neighborhood, it was agreed that the extra space for an addition, required by the program, would be found at the side of the library by closing a side street. To maintain the balance and symmetry of the historic structure, and to restrain the mass of the main steel and glass addition, the original fabric was extended with two small brick additions as bookends to the original building. One was added on the north side, modifying a small one-story addition built in 1900; the other on the south side, mirroring it, and connecting to the new space. This allowed the original two-story Doric portico entrance to remain the dominant element of the building, and its main point of entry.

Extra space in the original building was also reclaimed from the basement by lowering the floor 3 feet. Because of the sloping topography of the site, this level leads into above-ground space in the new addition. The children's library is at this level, opening onto a reading garden designed in an informal, almost rural character. Rocks excavated from the site are carved with a children's poem by A.A. Milne, 'Now We Are Six,' and provide casual seating for all ages.

Interior finishes are designed to create a sense of continuity between historic and modern while also emphasizing their differences. The overall effect is one of a counterpoint where each part informs a sympathetic reading of the other.

1 Joining of old and new library wings
2 New reading area is partially a double-height space
3 Glazed walls of addition reveal contents

6

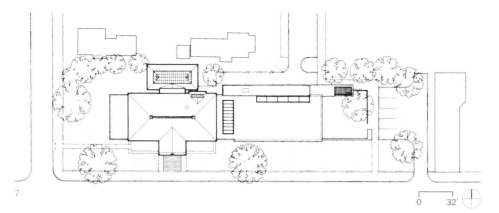

4 Glassy new addition contrasts with masonry elder

5 Glassy seminar rooms offer privacy for group study

6 Reading garden with rocks carved with verse

7 Site plan

8 Original building's restored reading room

7

0   32'

8

9

10

9 Reading and stack areas in addition
10 Connection of old library to new wing
11 Original details were carefully restored
12 Light colors and materials lift the space
photography: Steve Rosenthal

Multnomah County Central Library

Fletcher Farr Ayotte PC (Executive Architect)
Hardy Holzman Pfeiffer Associates (Associate Architect)

The rehabilitated and expanded 125,000-square-foot Multnomah County Central Library is one of Portland's best-loved landmarks. The original 1913 building was designed by A.E. Doyle, a leading architect of the era, and is listed on the National Register of Historic Places. A classic example of Georgian revival architecture, the structure occupies a full block in downtown Portland.

Working with George MeMath, grandson of A.E. Doyle and an architect himself, the architects identified key elements for restoration. Historic photographs showed original conditions and furnishings in the major lobby spaces and reading rooms, as well as giving craftspeople a source for recreating several historic light fixtures.

A new series of vestibules and lobby spaces at the front door allows direct access to a multipurpose meeting room, The Friends of the Library store, and new 'welcome' desk. Much of the first floor is now devoted to public use, with a greatly expanded children's library that includes a new storytelling and program area, and a larger popular library featuring a coffee bar as well as current bestsellers. New fourth and fifth floors have been discretely added to the building to accommodate a new administrative and staff center; nearly a quarter of the floor area in the building is new construction.

continued

1 Exterior after restoration and rehabilitation
photography: Hoffman Construction
opposite: Grand staircase from second to third floor
photography: Jeff Krausse

The interior design of the library blends the classic Georgian approach to decoration with the library's overall theme of 'The Garden of Knowledge.' The public spaces on each floor are distinguished by pastel colors: yellow, rose, and blue; white tones highlight the room's ceiling and window trim; extensive use of new wood trim and shelving lend warmth to the lobby and reading areas. Reading tables are typically placed near windows to take advantage of natural light. Working with artist Larry Kirkland, the design team wove the motifs of the surrounding Northwest National Forests and the theme of discovery into all aspects of the building.

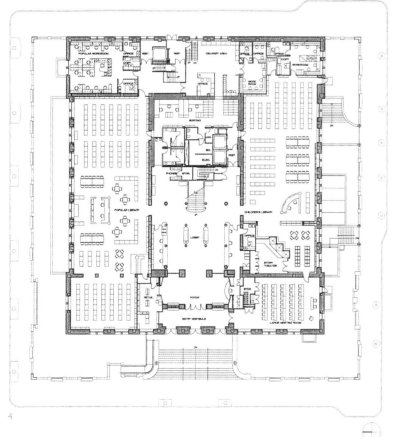

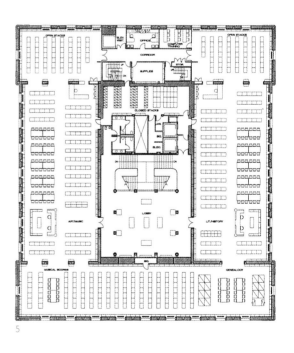

3 Lobby at first floor

photography: Foaad Farah

4 First floor plan

5 Third floor plan

6 Custom reading tables and chairs

photography: Sally Painter

7 Children's library on first floor

photography: Laurie Black

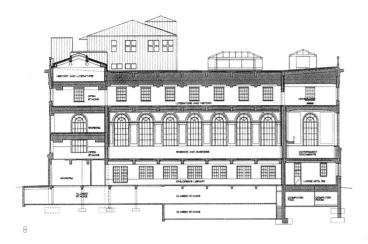

8

9

10

11

8 East–west building section

9 Grand staircase at second floor lobby

photography: Andre Bodo

10 Third floor lobby

11 Second floor reading room

photography: Foaad Farah

Timberland North Mason Public Library

Carlson Architects

This new 15,000-square-foot library occupies a site on the main street of Belfair, Washington that is heavily wooded and backs up to a dense wetland forest that extends to nearby Hood Canal.

The design concept for the new library was to make a building 'in and of the forest,' a structure that would take its design cues from the woods. The library was to be a civic landmark that would reflect the timbering heritage of Belfair. The building was sited to maintain the maximum number of existing mature evergreen trees.

The structure's organization resembles a tight-knit compound of separate building elements linked by a tall central circulation spine. The separate elements include the main reading room block, the children's library and meeting room block, and the staff work area block.

Interior spaces are oriented into the surrounding forest and large windows in sitting and reading areas provide views deep into the woods. Other windows lift high above the roofline to heighten the forest views and offer craning glimpses up into tree canopies. A large window at the end of the main reading room protrudes beyond the space into the forest domain. A mysterious stick-tree-framed opening beckons children into the storytelling nook—a glass room looking out into the forest.

Simple exterior materials such as concrete block, and ribbed metal wall and roof cladding are reminiscent of local mill building construction. Black split-face concrete block and dark green metal roofs make the building appear to recede into the forest like tree trunks or dark shadows. Weathered silver galvanized-metal cladding on the spine roof and main reading room walls glistens in the light, calling attention to the library. On the interior, large timber trusses support the roof of the main reading room and of the circulation spine. The spine is reminiscent of a mill-run shed. High clerestory windows fill the spine with natural light giving the impression of an open-air shed.

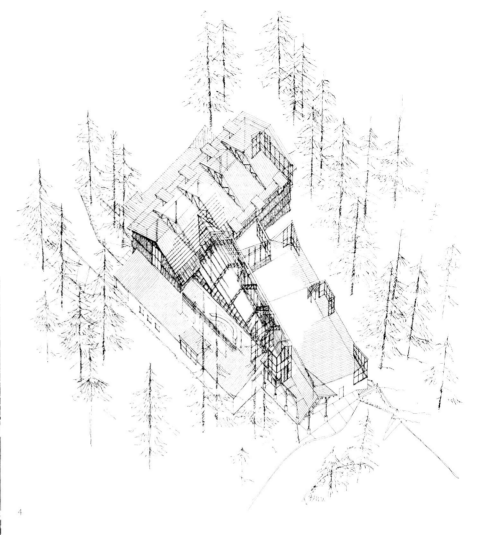

1 Exterior is a combination of metal siding and glass areas
2 Building blends in with the wooded site
3 Interior is alive with warm wood materials
4 Sketch
5 Exterior suggests mill buildings of the region

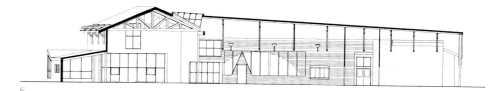

6

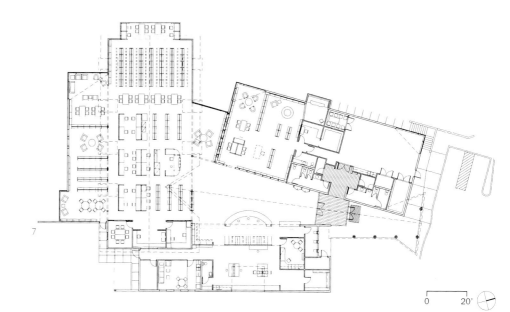

7

0   20'

8

9

10

11

12

John Deaver Drinko Library
Marshall University

Perry Dean Rogers | Partners Architects

This 125,000-square-foot structure houses over 200,000 volumes and incorporates traditional library functions with state-of-the-art computer education facilities that include multimedia training and presentation rooms, over 1000 work stations, and the information technology center for the entire Marshall University campus in Huntington, West Virginia.

The library is conceived symbolically as the marriage of traditional library functions represented by the more historical and contextual brick façades that hark back to Old Main, the most venerable building on campus, with that of newer, computer-based research methods as represented by the glass, steel, and stucco portions of the exterior. The central rotunda cylinder acts as the bridge between these two ideas as well as the main entry to the facility. A stainless-steel canopy arcs along a pedestrian path and connects back in the entry cylinder with a wavy tongue that passes through the glass walls and hovers over the circulation desk.

Inside, the library's spaces are arranged with a logic that places people near windows and open vistas, while the collection and computer spaces reside at the building's heart.

There is a 24-hour reading room/computer lab with consultation rooms and workstations, and notebooks running on an ultra-fast telecommunications backbone. The collection includes books and bound periodicals, with a wide variety of media- and Internet-accessible electronic materials. The facility has study rooms, conference collaboration rooms, an auditorium with distance learning capabilities, and a ground-floor café. The information technology center on the top floor contains offices for university libraries, instructional technology, university computing services, and telecommunications.

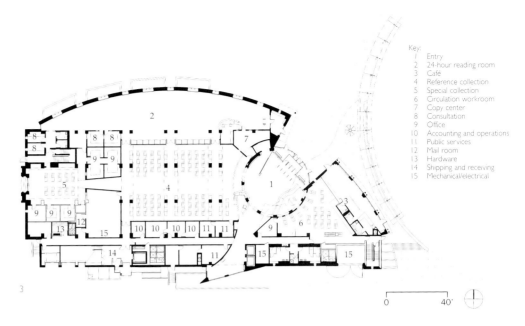

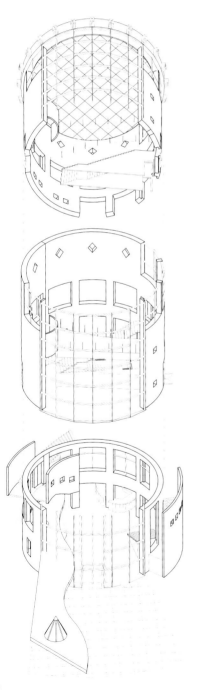

1 View of library from north

2 View into 24-hour reading room

3 First floor plan

4 View of reference desk in main lobby

5 Main entry in double-height space

6 Axonometric

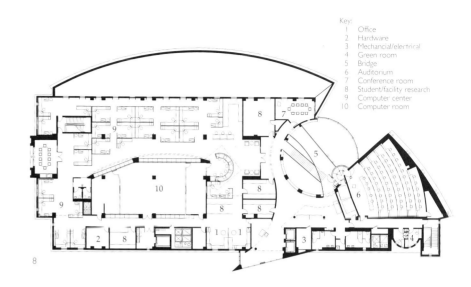

8

7

9

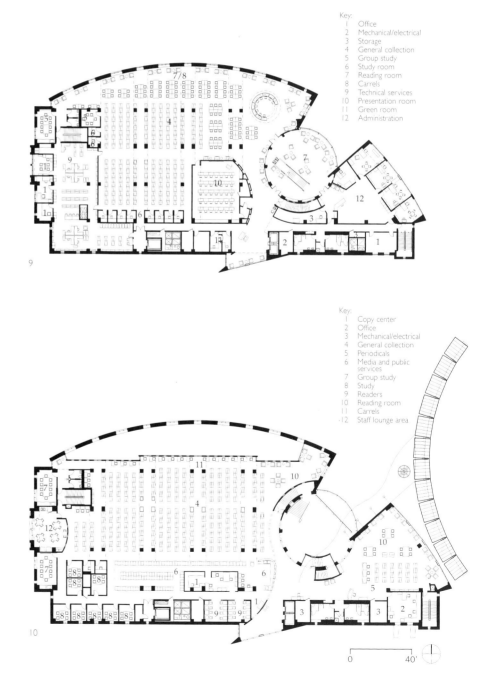

10

0   40'

11   12

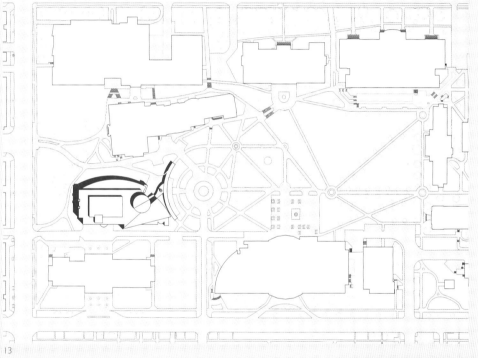

13

14   15

7   Curves are used to define pathways

8   Fourth floor plan

9   Third floor plan

10 Second floor plan

11 View of building's upper atrium

12 Computer terminal in reading lounge

13 Site plan

14 Building uses materials akin to other
     university buildings

15 Auditorium is found on fourth floor

photography: Richard Mandelkorn

Kansas Center for Historical Research

ASAI Architecture

The Kansas State Historical Society in Topeka, Kansas is the repository for Kansas lore, prairie artifacts, and archives historic documents. It provides a public library for historical research and education facilities to increase public accessibility.

For almost 80 years, it was housed in a grand but unremarkable neoclassical building near the state capitol in Topeka. In 1984, the state constructed a new history museum on an open prairie site next to the historic 1848 Potawattomie Indian-Baptist Mission. Beside the mission and the museum, the new Center for Historical Research, housing the state archives, research library, and the Kansas Historical Society headquarters, takes its place.

In one stroke, the new center recomposes the entire site and relationship of existing buildings, to create a unified campus that uses the historic mission as a focal element. The center connects to the existing museum forming a 'U' configuration that frames a central outdoor space for the historical society's 'living history forum.' The original parking area is relocated away from the mission presenting a more natural setting and allowing restoration of a historic wagon trail. The existing canopy system is extended from the new parking area to the center's entrance providing a transitional buffer that screens awkward architectural differences between museum and mission. The composition's new approach from the east, honors the mission as a symbolic entrance gateway.

The center's architectural form derives from both the mission and the museum. The new building's scale, gabled roof form, clerestory infill between roof and walls, and window fenestration in the stone walls, all echo the mission's vernacular architecture in contemporary vocabulary. The limestone walls are direct extensions of the museum using the same height, material, and joinery.

Inspired by the mission's scale and structure, the basic planning unit is a simple, economical 30-foot compartmentalized storage module. It repeats and grows to form the overall building, and supports an incremental expansions plan. The design system adapts morphologically to increased spans and special requirements of public spaces creating environments reminiscent of the Great Plains pole barns.

3

4

1 Mission building is wrapped by newer structures

2 View of building from northeast

3 Entrance into center

4 Walkway to center is covered for weather protection

opposite: View from lobby into reading room

6 Entry lobby is light and welcoming

7 Specially designed light fixtures

8 North wall of reading room

photography: Assassi Productions

6

7

8

Vancouver Central Public Library

Moshe Safdie Associates
Downs Archambault & Partners

Containing the city's central public library, a federal office tower, and retail and service facilities, Library Square occupies a city block in the eastward expansion of the downtown core of Vancouver, British Columbia. Designed as a public place with a civic identity, Library Square is an open and inviting addition to the heart of the city.

Centered on the block, the 350,000-square-foot library is a seven-story rectangular box containing book stacks and services, surrounded by a free-standing elliptical colonnaded wall containing reading and study areas that are accessed by bridges spanning skylit lightwells. The library's internal glass façade overlooks an enclosed concourse formed by a second elliptical wall that defines the east side of the site.

This generous, glass-roofed concourse serves as an entry foyer to the library and creates a dialogue between the contemplative spaces of the library and the more lively pedestrian activities at ground level. The arcaded wall of the concourse ascends to a 21-story height to the northeast, forming one face of the federal office tower and creating continuity between the two structures.

The public spaces surrounding the library form a continuous piazza with parking located below grade. The building is clad in sandstone-colored precast concrete. The northeast bay of the office tower is completely glazed to form a dramatic bay window with views toward the city and the harbor. With its scale, materials, and civic presence, this library defines a landmark at the city's heart and marries a place of learning with a place of commerce.

1 Library has a strong urban presence

2 Carrels are placed near light and views

3 Overlooking exterior plaza, interior courtyard, and reading areas

4 Library reaches out to welcome visitors

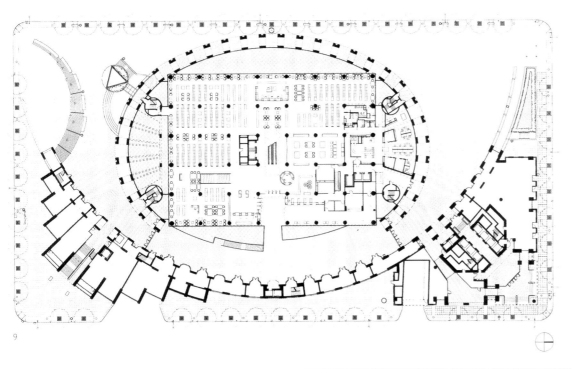

9

10

5 Promenade areas on upper levels

6 Multistory concourse is an important civic space

7 Corridors embrace library's stack areas

8 View of stack areas under glass roof

9 Ground floor plan

10 Library occupies a city block with office
tower in background

photography: Timothy Hursley

Library/Media Center
Glendale Community College
Richärd & Bauer Architecture

1

The Library Media Center is a renovation of an existing mid-1960s media center/classroom building into a state-of-the-art library/media center. The 38,000-square-foot building was completely gutted, and the center court and southern entry were enclosed to capture an additional 4000 square feet of space. The project's program includes a collection of 112,000 volumes, an expansive reading room, group study and distance learning classrooms, audiovisual presentation studio, media viewing/audio center, instructional support center, collaborative learning classroom, and a 50-seat computer commons space.

The building entry sequence was completely reoriented to the east and west, activating the main pedestrian mall. The project is organized by a series of layered shells around and within the existing building. Each shell modulates light in a different way, alternately shading, concealing, revealing, and obscuring spaces within, with the changing light. An outdoor courtyard and sculpture garden is designed to the south of the building with access through a large reading room. Cantilevered glass walls enclose the existing flower columns, maximizing the openness and impact of the campus icon. This relationship to the context is further reinforced by the use of weathered steel panels, which recall the campus use of terracotta masonry.

The existing cast-in-place concrete structure is the ideal foil for the light and delicate intrusions of the design. The raw texture of the existing structure is revealed within the space, drawing contrast between the old and the new. Two large hand-troweled plaster walls are the backdrop for the school's extensive art collection. Use of a notched trowel finish creates a surface that changes with light and the angle of view. These walls contain the collection within and separate the primary space from support and staff areas at the perimeter of the building.

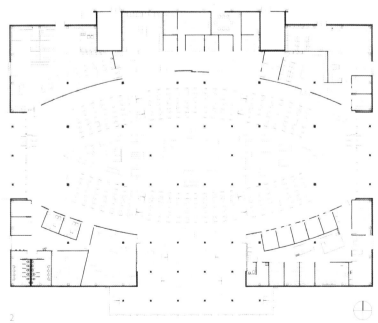

2

1 Screen wall in front of library
2 Floor plan
3 Screens temper views into reading areas
4 Detail of exterior, with light monitor above
5 Glass wall is shaded with overhang to modulate sunlight

3

4

5

6

7

8

6 Interior plaster walls reveal pattern of hand-troweling

7 Screen wall directs visitors to library entry

8 Interior of newly refurbished library

9 Library's lighting is modulated with exterior screens

10 Light monitor over computer area

11 Detail of sunscreen overhang

photography: Bill Timmerman

9

10

11

Rakow Research Library
Corning Museum of Glass

Bohlin Cywinski Jackson

Designed in response to the need for a secure environment for the storage of the library's irreplaceable collection of written and graphic information on the history of glass, carefully controlled environmental requirements were set for this archival environment. Also important was the need to protect the collections from the threat of floods. Conservation requirements were carefully balanced with accessibility to collections and reader friendliness.

Originally housed within Corning's Museum of Glass building, the continually expanding collections necessitated relocation. After various sites on the Corning Campus were evaluated, it was decided to place the library within the shell of a vacant and mundane 1966 office building.

The project took the form of a radical reconstruction including significant reinforcement of the steel structure to place the collections upstairs, protecting them from potential flood damage. This restructuring afforded several design opportunities, including openings in the second floor linking upper and lower levels in a linear atrium. Mechanical and electrical infrastructure was entirely replaced to accommodate advanced archival systems. In addition to very narrow temperature and humidity tolerances, these systems incorporate elaborate air quality controls, a fire suppression system designed to minimize potential water damage, and careful segregation of heating and plumbing piping to avoid the risk of leaks in collections areas. Interior finishes were chosen to minimize the introduction of airborne contaminants.

continued

1 Decorative construction marks entrance
2 Light is filtered by screen on south elevation
3 Light screen on south elevation softens light
4 Section/elevation

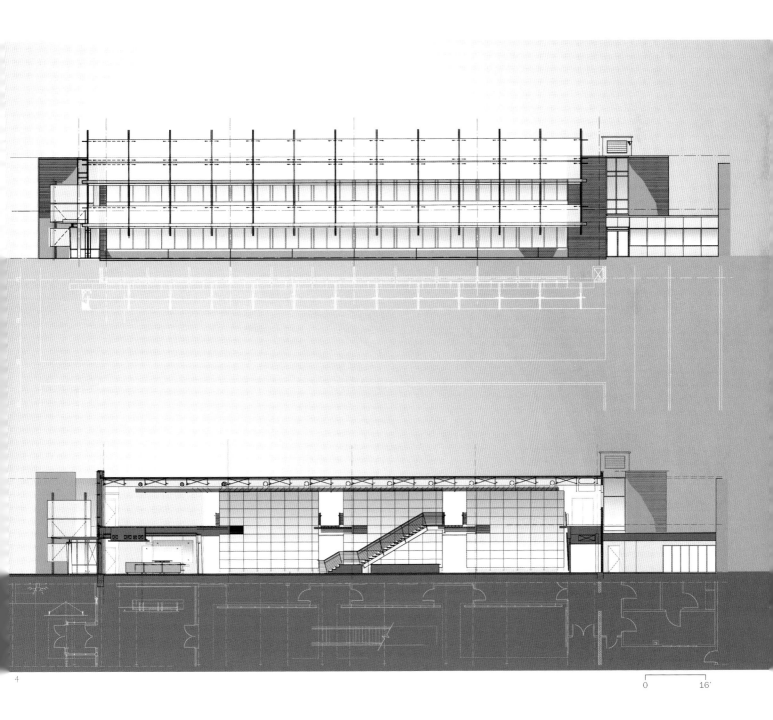

4

0   16'

The design expresses the fact that the library is an adaptation of an older structure. Within this context, the new library celebrates glass, thematically relating the building to the collection's subject matter and to the museum's nearby Glass Center. Glass detailing characterizes the 'building within a building' where the collections are housed, as well as special features such as glass-floored stairs and bridges. The south-facing reading areas enjoy a river view through a glass brise soleil. This sunscreen serves as a large environmental sculpture, transforming the character of the former office building. Its ceramic-frit and acid-etched linear patterns interact with seasonal sun angles to maximize visual transparency while excluding direct sunlight from the library's interior.

5

5 Public reading room on second floor

opposite: Staircase in reception/exhibit area

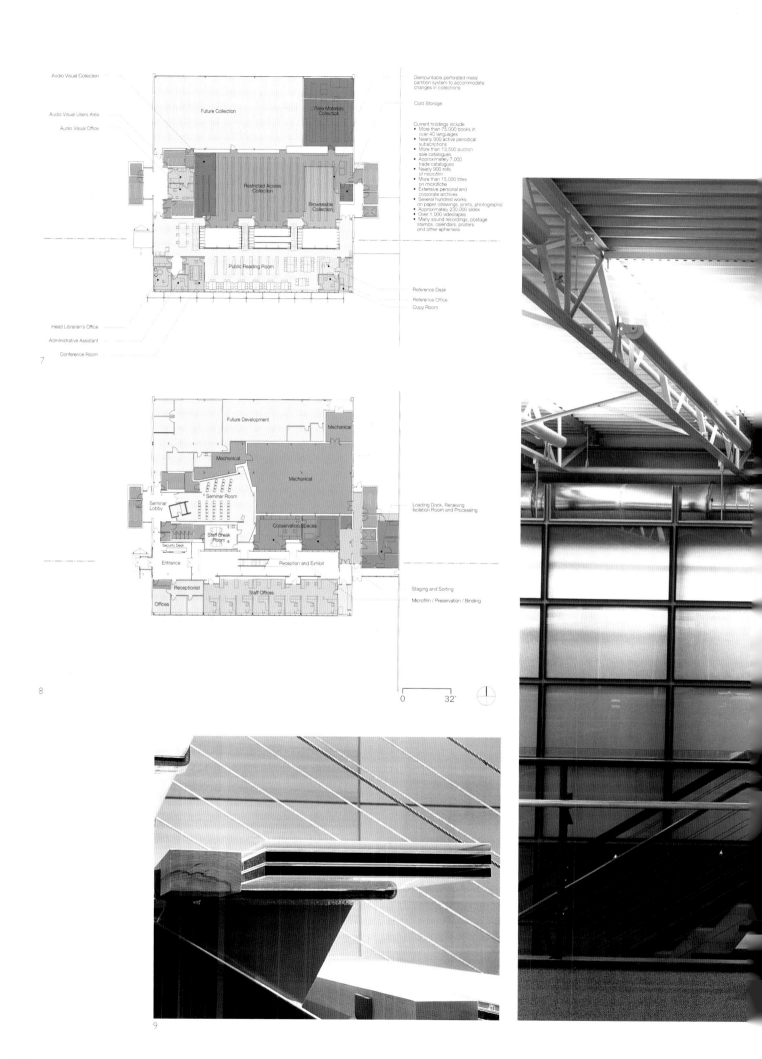

Audio Visual Collection

Audio Visual Users Area

Audio Visual Office

Future Collection

Rare Materials Collection

Restricted Access Collection

Browseable Collection

Public Reading Room

Head Librarian's Office

Administrative Assistant

Conference Room

7

Demountable perforated metal
partition system to accommodate
changes in collections

Cold Storage

Current holdings include
• More than 75,000 books in
  over 40 languages
• Nearly 900 active periodical
  subscriptions
• More than 13,500 auction
  sale catalogues
• Approximately 7,000
  trade catalogues
• Nearly 900 rolls
  of microfilm
• More than 15,000 titles
  on microfiche
• Extensive personal and
  corporate archives
• Several hundred works
  on paper (drawings, prints, photographs)
• Approximately 230,000 slides
• Over 1,000 videotapes
• Many sound recordings, postage
  stamps, calendars, posters
  and other ephemera

Reference Desk

Reference Office

Copy Room

Future Development

Mechanical

Mechanical

Mechanical

Seminar Room

Seminar
Lobby

Conservation Spaces

Staff Break
Room

Security Desk

Entrance

Reception and Exhibit

Receptionist

Offices

Staff Offices

8

Loading Dock, Receiving
Isolation Room and Processing

Staging and Sorting

Microfilm / Preservation / Binding

0   32'

9

10

Bend Public Library

Thomas Hacker Architects

This public library in Bend is located in a small, rapidly growing city in central Oregon at the base of the Cascade Mountains. Sited on the city's main street and across from the primary downtown public space, Heritage Square, the building is a key ingredient in plans to rejuvenate the city's historic downtown area. The design was based on the understanding that this was to be a truly civic space for the city's residents and visitors; a place that was entirely accessible, putting the library's resources clearly in the hands of the public.

The design starts with a formal alignment of the building, including the entrance, with the axis of the square. The city axis extends through a generous lobby to a large open stair, which draws visitors up to the main reading room on the second floor. This is an open timber-framed lodge-like space with clerestory light and large glazed openings to expansive views of the mountains and the activity in Heritage Square below.

The main space is a room of natural wood and natural light, set within and on top of the heavier masonry block that defines the library's boundaries and projects its civic stature. The central bay of the reading room is lifted above the surrounding roof and stretches across its entire length, bringing natural light deep into the space's center. The long axis of the room, simultaneously formal in aspect and informal in scale, is completed at either end by dramatic views of the magnificent mountain and desert landscape in which Bend is situated.

Local materials and crafts are used exclusively throughout both interior and exterior. The stone in the walls is quarried nearby, the brick is manufactured in a regional factory and all timber is from mills in the area, further linking the building to its place. These traditional local materials are reworked within a modern architectural vocabulary to give the building a modern sensibility, grounded in and respectful of the traditions of local building.

2

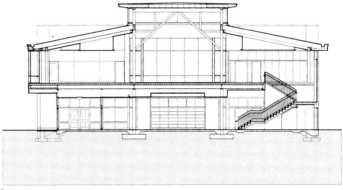

3

1 Materials are simple yet elegant
2 Central axis of upper reading room
3 Cross section
4 Exterior has a civic bearing

photography: John Hughel

4

Peninsula Center Library Renovation and Addition

Zimmer Gunsul Frasca Partnership

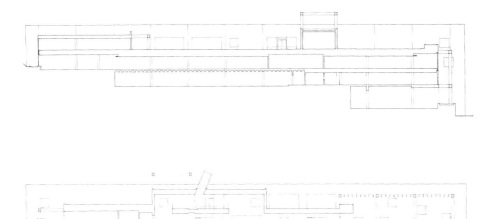

This library in Rolling Hills Estates, California, originally designed by architect Quincy Jones in the 1960s, had outgrown its former capacity. The library needed to double its space requirements and update its accessibilty, improve lighting, reduce energy consumption, and comply with current health and safety regulations.

The existing concrete-frame building, on a steeply sloped site between two arterial streets, contains four levels: a main library level, an upper rooftop parking level, an administrative office/partially underground parking level, and the Silver Spur entrance/underground parking level.

The design solution maintains the entrance at the upper street, which continues to be served by rooftop parking, and adds a new entrance on the main street below. A curved wall slices through all levels and acts as the principal orienting device

2

for the entire building. Painted bright yellow, this shear wall links the addition to the old structure, reducing the quantity of shear walls needed in the existing building and maintaining an open plan. This yellow wall also separates the public entrance galleries and meeting rooms from the controlled access zone of the library work areas. Upon entering the library, one passes through the curved wall and is oriented to the circulation and reference desks beyond. At the outer edges, reading areas are located at the perimeter windows.

Covering most of the site, the building mass is minimized by layers of trellis—horizontal on the upper street and vertical on the lower. The street façades are a series of layered scrims made of perforated blinds, patterned glass, landscape, and trellis that filters light and maintains privacy for reading areas adjacent to the street, while allowing visibility to the activities within.

A competitive art program resulted in a collaboration of artist and architect that was integral to the building design. Lita Albuquerque's *Stellar Axis* penetrates all four levels of the library's public entrance galleries, while Gwynne Murrill's bronze cheetahs and stone column carved with endangered animals create an atmosphere that is welcoming and enlivening for children.

3

1 Section
2 Library's north elevation
3 View of building from northwest

4 Circulation desk is welcoming
5 Third floor is light with warm
    wood tones
6 Second floor plan
7 Part of entry lobby
8 First floor plan

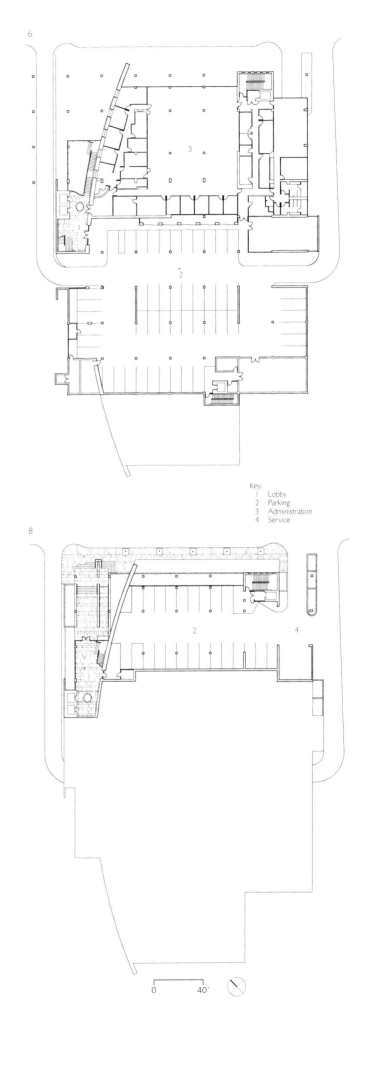

Key:
1 Lobby
2 Parking
3 Administration
4 Service

0   40'

Peninsula Center Library Renovation and Addition 177

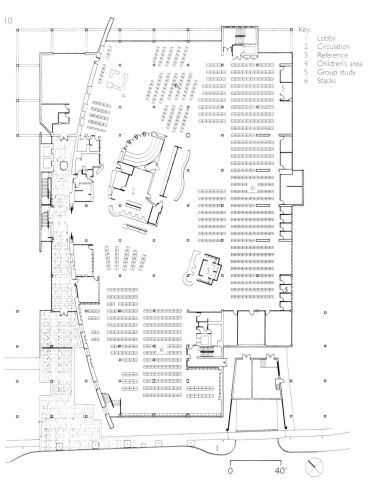

10

Key:
1 Lobby
2 Circulation
3 Reference
4 Children's area
5 Group study
6 Stacks

0   40'   ⊗

opposite: Natural materials give warmth to interiors

10 Third floor plan

11 Third floor stack and reading areas

12 Second floor lobby

photography: Nick Merrick/Hedrich-Blessing

11

12

Daniel Mannix Library
Catholic Theological College

Gregory Burgess Architects

The Catholic Theological College moved from Clayton to inner Melbourne, Victoria, Australia with the goal of heightening its profile, reviewing its aims and image with the turn of the 21st century. The chosen site is rich with history. It was the former home of Parade College and later Cathedral College and it was to be cleared of all existing structures other than an 1870s neo-Gothic bluestone building. Being a heritage-listed building, the relationship between the old and the new was critical.

The new design creates a 'dance' between the old and new. The space between the two buildings allows them both dignity, as expressions of their time. A transparent connection links the buildings at two levels and allows the new to grow out of the old. From this point, the fluid structure unfolds in a powerful curve. Located in the center of the site is a highly symbolic courtyard that can be viewed from all aspects of the college, as well as contemplated from within.

Occupying an upper level of the new building, the Daniel Mannix Library is the heart of the new college, with its magnificent collection of historic manuscripts and books and excellent study facilities. The books fill a large internal space protected from direct sunlight. Around the edge of the book storage is the circulation area, a low space with windows fanning like the pages of a book. They frame many vignettes of the old building, the courtyard, and the street trees. A rhythmic undulating ceiling moves over them, gathering the space as it rolls westward rising into the light-filled mezzanine.

Light is an important physical and psychological element in the building, its quality being critical in creating an appropriate ambience for working and well being. On the edge of the curving area between the circulation and book storage is a series of ceiling openings modulating daylight to study carrels below. An extensive skylight runs the length of the mezzanine directing light down into the library workroom as well as into the mezzanine itself.

1 Courtyard of the new building
2 Entry to building as it faces Eade Street
3 Multi-height drum space over entry
4 Light-filled reading spaces
5 Main entry to building, next to historic structure
photography: John Gollings

3

4

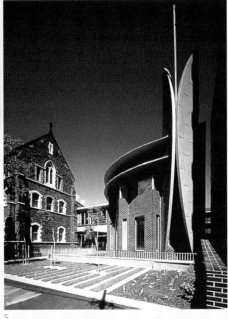

5

Johnson County Central Resource Library

Gould Evans

This central resource library in Overland Park, Kansas replaces an outdated and undersized main branch library and technical services facility. Orientation, accessibility, and flexibility for technological growth, and expression of function were the primary goals set forth by the client. Within 85,000 square feet under a 20-foot roof structure, the interior architecture had to contend with awkward proportions. The design is rooted within the precedent of a village. Two primary corridors create main streets that divide the interior into neighborhoods. The intersecting main streets are highly differentiated, one a vaulted, broad space punctuated by a rhythm of steel rafters and very softly lit, the other narrow and soaring to a skylit roof, pouring light into the center of the building.

At the intersection of the two main streets is the forum, which functions as the town square. Strong daylight from all directions reinforces the space's conceptual connection to traditional outdoor public squares, while projecting a glowing beacon to the community by night. This focal point is a place for welcoming the public, an area for social interchange, and a place for information and exhibition.

Brightly colored landmarks, housing conference rooms and offices, are placed throughout the neighborhoods to help define street edges, gateways, and enclosure for private space. The main landmark signifies the information services desk. The ceiling is cut out over this space in an oval shape, and suspended within is a wood and plate aluminum grid.

Located in a former discount retail store, this state-of-the-art library uses in-floor wiring ducts throughout the public service area for ultimate flexibility in arranging furniture while providing power and data connections. The lighting system is arranged in a 'universal' pattern utilizing low-cost fixtures that provide superior illumination for any arrangement of reading tables, stacks, and computer stations.

continued

2

3

Reuse of the existing structure made economic and environmental sense. Tons of natural resources and energy embodied in the existing building were saved. Materials used in the building were selected for their minimal impact on the environment.

4

5

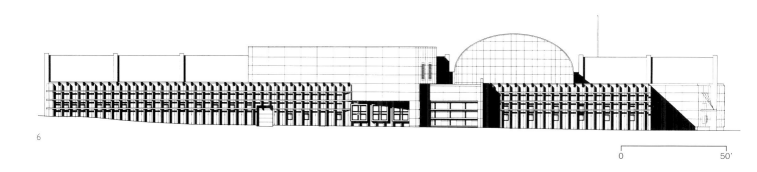

6

0   50'

7

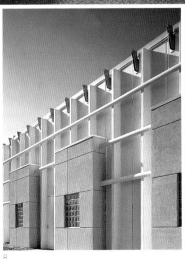

4 Reading areas along glazed wall

5 Entry is welcoming and light-filled

6 Section looking north

7 Conference rooms, on left, are found
  near reading areas

8 Detail of east elevation

9 Glass-block wall allows penetration of light

8   9

10

10 Vibrant colors enliven interiors

11 A variety of light sources are found within

opposite: Corridors are bright with skylights above

photography: Mike Sinclair

11

Carmel Mountain Ranch Community Library

M.W. Steele Group

Carmel Mountain Ranch is a new planned community of approximately 50,000 residents in the northeast region of San Diego, California. The Carmel Mountain Ranch Community Library is approximately 13,000 square feet, containing a general collection, reference collection, media collection, children's library, community room, and support spaces.

The library is sited at the edge of the retail-oriented town center, affording views of the foothills to the east, with the town center to the west. Directly south is a residential neighborhood and to the north is the fire station.

The library is designed with a large main space containing all the collections except for the children's, which is located in one of the wings at the west end of the main building. The building is articulated at the entrance, defining the pedestrian entrances from the street corner and the parking lot. This articulation also allows for separate access after hours to the community rooms and their supporting facilities.

The main space is surrounded and enclosed by glass. Windows, both operable and fixed, comprise this glass enclosure. Browsing, reading in lounge seating, or studying in the carrels is greatly enhanced by the sense of being in a garden pavilion. Natural light and views to the surrounding hills create this experience.

continued

1 Axial view from courtyard through stacks
2 View of library from northwest
3 Courtyard is behind high wall
4 Reading porch is protected by roof

The garden wall that contains the surrounding outdoor space is broken periodically with artistic fixed gates designed by the architects and fabricated by artisans in nearby Tijuana, Mexico. These breaks add visual interest and views both in and out of the garden. The garden contains native plant materials, a lawn, and intimate seating areas for reading and discussion.

The overall building form with a V-shaped roof is derived from a fitting together of the desires to create natural cross ventilation, shield the glass from direct sunlight, and fill the space with natural light. Natural cross-ventilation helps to cool the building even on the most severe days because avoiding direct sunlight reduces the heat load from the sun. Abundant natural light reduces the need for artificial lighting.

opposite: Entry to circulation area
6 Section
7 Site plan

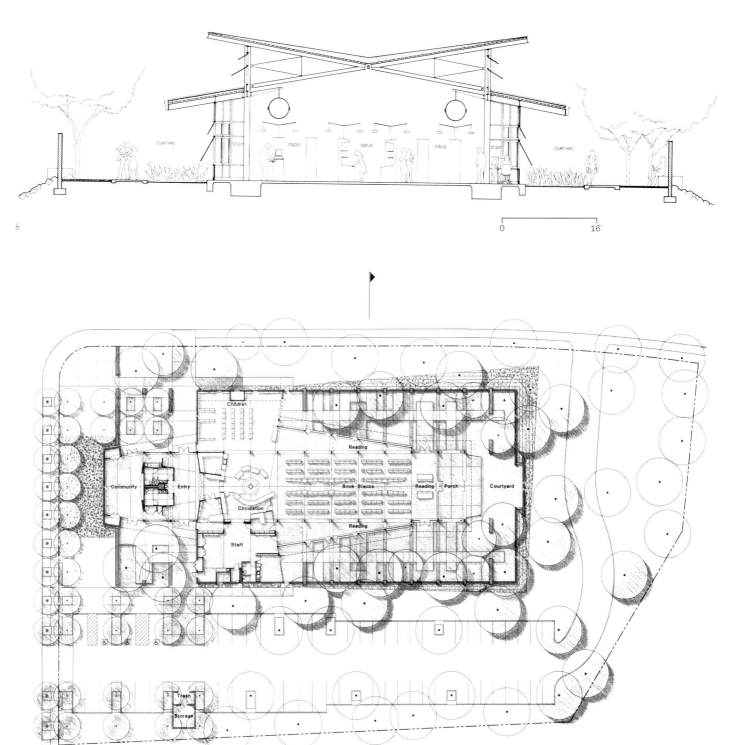

6

0   16'

7

0   64'

8

9

8 Green areas near building entry

9 Reading areas are at the library's glassy periphery

10 View of circulation area and stacks

11 Sunny areas are welcome for reading areas

12 Axial view down through stacks

photography: David Hewitt/Anne Garrison

Health Sciences and Human Services Library University of Maryland

Perry Dean Rogers | Partners Architects
Design Collective (Joint Venture Architect)

The new Health Sciences and Human Services Library at the University of Maryland in Baltimore (UMB) is one of the most sophisticated library/information technology centers in the country. The 190,000-square-foot building serves the UMB health and human services professional campus, a specialized training ground for physicians, dentists, pharmacists, lawyers, and nurses.

The library has a bulky, urban presence. It is a masculine object rendered in lasting materials of brick, limestone, and steel (the building's visual weight is reduced with the lavish use of the light-colored stone on its principal façades). These same materials are found in the library's context, and the new ties tightly to what is already there.

A heavily computer-driven building, the new facility merges the traditional library with the computer science department of the university. The combination of information services with the library encourages collaboration in the creation, assembly, storage, retrieval, and transmission of information. Students are able to gain access to information by plugging their laptop computers into dataports distributed throughout the building.

At the building's heart is its most monumental space—a dramatic staircase that rises five stories in contiguous runs. This is a powerful unifying device that stitches the multitude of library spaces together. It helps orient the visitor, who can easily move from one level to another. And it becomes an important social space where people meet in their journey through the library.

Other components of the building include administrative offices, classrooms, computer laboratories, and demonstration rooms, as well as display and storage space for the university's collection of rare and historical medical books, and a large meeting and special-events room.

1 Entry to library from west
2 Openings look out onto lobby space
3 Colorful aperture in curved wall
4 Library as it addresses its busy corner

2

3

4

5

6

Barrington Library
Addition and Renovation

Ross Barney + Jankowski Architects

1

Barrington, Illinois recognized the need for a major building addition to its public library. Besides generalized expansion, the expanded library program included a new large public meeting room. The original library was a low-profile brick and tile building that nestled into a heavily wooded site. The new design seeks to maintain the original ambience while improving views from the building into the site and enhancing the library's identity from a heavily trafficked highway.

The 30,700-square-foot addition is part of a comprehensive expansion/renovation project that essentially doubled the size of the library.

The new plan joins the new and old building elements along an arcaded 'street' leading patrons from the parking lot to the hospitality/welcome desk. The main 'street' is intersected by a secondary axis directly in front of the hospitality desk. This 'street' takes patrons to the major library service nodes: circulation, adult, reference, and young people's services. Meeting rooms are also on the axis.

The new entry space is one of the most exciting elements of the expanded building. From a distance, this welcoming space provides a sense of mystery and is enclosed by a wood structure. Closely spaced columns built from dimension lumber reach up like tree limbs to support light, wood-framed joists, visually joining it to the woods surrounding the building on the site. Daylight from clerestory windows filters through the welcoming branch-like structure to the lobby floor below. Other building materials used in the addition match the original palette.

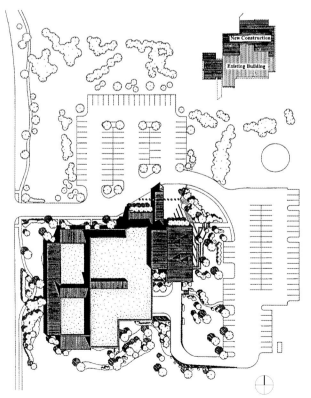

2

1 Small plaza in front of library provides a gathering space

2 Site plan

opposite: Axis down main entry is a veritable forest

4 View of main entry hall from south

5 Detail of entry canopy and main entry hall structure

6 View of library from northwest

7 Entry canopy roof echoes that of main entry hall

8 Courtyard just outside multipurpose room

9 Detail of columns and struts supporting roof

11

opposite: Multipurpose room has views out to site

11 Children's area uses bright colors and bold shapes

12 Main entry hall glows with structure at night

13 Second floor plan

14 First floor plan

photography: Steve Hall/Hedrich-Blessing

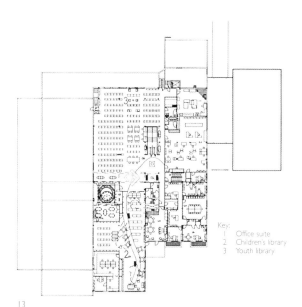

Key:
1   Office suite
2   Children's library
3   Youth library

13

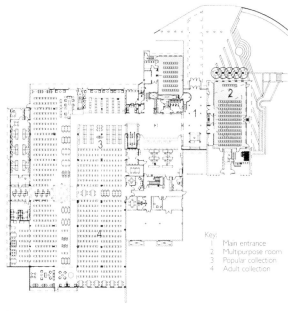

Key:
1   Main entrance
2   Multipurpose room
3   Popular collection
4   Adult collection

14

12

Los Feliz Branch Library
Barton Phelps & Associates

This library shares a busy intersection with the small buildings and big signs of two mini-malls and a gas station—the middle landscape of Los Angeles. Nestled beneath Griffith Park, the site drops along noisy Hillhurst Avenue to give long views of downtown and the sprawling cityscape to the south. Uphill views take in the craggy ridges of the park and the domes of its prominent 1930s observatory loom overhead.

Taking cues from the surrounding neighborhood where gridded blocks in the urban flats collide with curving, tree-lined streets on the hillsides, the building's form is hybrid. Its plan was informed by two contesting civic images as expressed by community members: one a formal urban presence to reinforce the street's pedestrian-friendly redevelopment, and the other a suburban public place—the library in the park—approached primarily by car. Both groups wanted the exterior to explain library function and welcome users of all ages.

The main volume abuts the sidewalk as a single story that steps back to rise to three stories when seen from a distance. At the corner, the glass-walled young adult's room mingles with the signs on other corners to mark the library's street entrance. Transparent during the day and illuminated at night, it invites teenagers to see in and be seen.

Within the site, a garden canopy of live oaks gives importance to the approach from parking. Building parts crunch together in the foyer where exterior paving and stucco walls flow through to link the flat-roofed block in front with low, shed-roofed volumes in the rear. Facing the dry garden that doubles as an outdoor theater, the turret of the storytelling room forms a stage backdrop and its trellis becomes a lighting grid.

The main reading room is an axial sequence of pyramidal, skylit bays that maximize natural light reflection to supply adequate illumination for daytime reading. Slit windows admit brighter slices of morning and afternoon light. In the children's storytelling room, daylight from the skylit vault filters through manzanita branches like a clearing in the chaparral above the library.

4

3

1 Detail of young adult area

2 West elevation is punctuated with pyramidal windows

3 Detail of storytelling room's exterior

4 Public artwork, The Conjunction of 500 Wishes, was worded with neighborhood help

5

6

5 Circulation area near children's room

6 Artwork in storytelling area

7 Section

8 View through main circulation area, looking north

9 Exterior corridor, which overlooks amphitheater

10 Section

photography: Tom Bonner

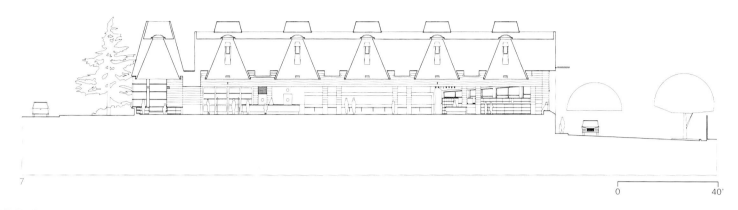

7

0   40'

8

9

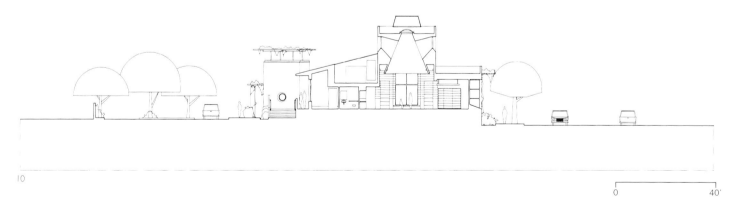

10

0   40'

School of Law Library
Seattle University

Olson Sundberg Kundig Allen Architects
Yost Grube Hall Architects (Associate Architects and Interior Designers)

The Seattle University School of Law reflects the university's commitment of service to the community, which is rooted in its Jesuit tradition. The desire to respond to this philosophy led to a design that connects the law school to the rest of the campus and to the larger community beyond. The new law school's contextual response is expressed primarily through the use of masonry and the emphasis on horizontal planes of fenestration.

Designed to accommodate approximately 840 students, the 136,000-square-foot school has an open atmosphere. Both faculty and students expressed a desire to be connected to each other visually. The new building responds with a multistory atrium space, from which all the major functions within the school are housed. This open quality also connects the building to the campus, and the window-wall system brings in generous amounts of daylight.

Within this open and inviting context is the law library. Given the library's large share of the building program, the challenge was to find ways to make this relatively hermetic element as open as possible. The massing of the library provides maximum exterior exposure with an open interior stair that connects all three levels of the library. The main library entry is found directly in front of the atrium space.

continued

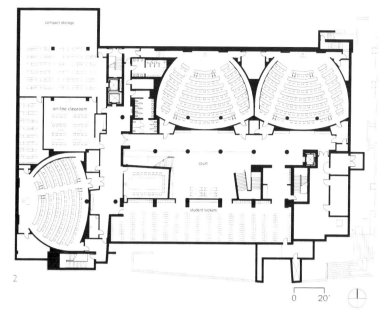

2

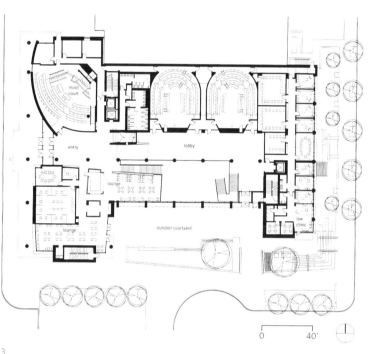

3

4

5

1 Detail of entrance to law school

2 Court floor plan

3 Main floor plan

4 View of entrance to law school, with glassy stair above

5 Law school building at night reveals its interior

Faculty and students debated the future of hard-copy texts, and what the growth trends for book acquisitions might be, given the advent of electronic data as the primary medium of legal research. The solution was to limit the hard-copy shelving space within the library proper as much as was practical, and to provide generous floor area for seating to accommodate on-line research. A wide variety of seating is available, from private carrels to team study workrooms to open tables and soft-seating areas, all with data-port and line voltage connections. To satisfy the inevitable growth in hard-copy media, a compact storage system was designed at a lower level to accommodate future expansion.

6

7

8

9

10

11

6 Sitting areas near atrium offer respite from studies

7 Detail of overhangs on law school's façade, with stair element to left

8 Library resource desk uses light wood

9 Open atrium is a gathering space for school community

10 Central stair is important element in library's interior

11 Natural light is delivered from clerestories above

photography: Benjamin Benschneider

Evanston Public Library

Nagle Hartray Dankar Kagan McKay (Architect of Record)
Joseph Powell (Design Architect)

The Evanston Public Library is designed to fulfill many missions. Its materials, their composition, and detailing echo an era of architectural enlightenment. The interior spaces are defined with clarity and simplicity. Yet, within the civic grandeur of an important 'community' space, patrons are able to explore the wonders of a library.

Taking advantage of its prominent location, at the intersection of two of main roads in Evanston, Illinois, the west and south façades of the new library are marked by a rhythm of brick and decorated cast-stone piers, creating a pattern of shade and light. The south façade features an entry plaza, landscaped on both sides, gradually rising to a monumental clock tower that marks the entrance. The central piers of the west façade, adorned with sculpture, open to reveal a curved metal roof over the main reference room beyond. The composition of the piers, sculpture, curved roof, clock tower, and entry plaza create a strong image, appropriate for such an important civic building. This design and the use of materials also suggest the early 20th-century work of Frank Lloyd Wright, a native Midwesterner. Echoes of Wright's Larkin Office Building and Unity Temple can be seen in the façades' design.

Inside, a vaulted-roofed main reference and reading room is filled with natural light and articulated materials, including Prairie style-inspired hanging light fixtures. Wood and steel details add to the domestic human scale of the library's interior.

1 Detail of library's main entry at night
2 Library has a strong civic presence
3 View of information area with art glass
4 Overview of reading area and periodicals

5 Light fixtures and furniture have Wright flavor

6 Reading area, including carrels, is light-filled

7 View of circulation desk

opposite: Central circulation space features a mobile

photography: Hedrich-Blessing

Carmel Clay Public Library

Meyer, Scherer, & Rockcastle

The Carmel Clay Public Library is designed to be an enduring yet dynamic civic resource for the residents of Clay Township, located in Carmel, Indiana. To accomplish this goal, a 113,600-square-foot library was designed and built to offer diverse spaces and modes of information for community students and residents of all ages.

The leading program requirement was for this public resource to incorporate the latest information technologies to meet educational objectives. As a solution, Carmel Clay Library provides numerous modes of information. More than 300,000 books and 655 periodicals with back issues are accessible to the public. Almost 46,000 non-print items such as CD-ROMs, video, and audiocassettes are also available here. And the latest information technologies are offered with over 120 on-line computer stations for public access to the catalog, Internet, and other databases.

As a dynamic civic resource, the library provides high-demand and high-interest material that also stimulates the interests and appreciation for reading and learning. The needs of a variety of users are addressed with special areas. For example, a 25,000-square-foot children's area includes a technology center, a large storytelling room, a puppet theater, two murals of nature scenes, a parent resource center, its own audiovisual collection, and three separate rooms for group study. The young adult area features books and computers specifically for teenagers. The adult area offers popular materials collections including bestsellers, magazines, tapes, and CD-ROMs, and an extensive business reference area is equipped with a nonfiction technology center.

continued

1 Library from the approach road
2 Curved glazed wall is light-filled
3 Detail of library entrance
4 Specially designed wood furniture
   accommodates library uses

4

To sustain this library as a dynamic place, it is designed to accommodate new, evolving formats. Secondly, it is built to serve with generous aisle widths, group study rooms, specialized lighting, and acoustic control. Finally, products were chosen according to their durability and maintenance requirements so that Carmel Clay Library can continue to be a public resource.

5

6

7

8

5 Color is used on the floor, with generous illumination
6 Sunny reading areas along walls with views
7 Café space has warm wood accents
8 Reading nooks offer a quiet place
9 View into reading and stack areas

photography: Bill Taylor of Taylor Photography

9

Langston Hughes Library

Maya Lin Studio
Martella Associates (Associate Architect)

1

This special collection library takes its place in a 'reborn' barn on Maley Farm in Clinton, Tennessee, breathing new life into the old structure. The barn dates from the 1860s. It is raised above grade and visually supported upon a log crib. The barn's structure, which was completely dismantled, is reconstructed to rest on the crib, which parts to allow entry to a skylit stair. Once inside, it immediately becomes apparent that the crib and barn are only exterior skins, and that a new building, independent of the old structures (which are exposed and essentially untouched), has been created within.

All of the interior spaces, materials, finishes, lighting, and equipment are new. For the most part, the historical outer skin and the new inner skin are independent of each other. At several points in the building, such as the glazed wall behind the crib logs, one becomes aware of the proximity of new to old. The crib walls are supported by a threaded steel rod, expressing this new structural element, instead of hiding it. One enters through a central opening in the crib, through a small garden room with a stone fountain. Once inside this lower space, the crib log walls can be read through the translucent glass of the new curtainwall within. On this level are a small bookstore, a stairway, and an elevator that beckon the visitor to the second level.

2

1 Salvaged barn becomes the host for the new library
2 Log construction can be read through translucent glass
3 Upper level reading room
4 Light-filled stair with translucent glass
5 Elegant, spare materials used in stair construction
photography: Timothy Hursley

4

Upstairs, the intimate spaces of the reading area and study area can be opened to each other to accommodate public gatherings for readings. Walls and ceilings are rendered in particleboard and maple, with skylights punctuating the entry stair, reading area, and stack area. Skylights are placed over the entry stair, the reading area with its large picture window, and stacks to increase the daylighting. Tabletops are made of recycled soybean husks, while the floors are covered with all-natural sisal carpeting.

3

5

Author and Contributor Notes

Michael J. Crosbie is an internationally recognized author, architect, journalist, critic, and teacher. A former editor of both *Progressive Architecture* and *Architecture*, he is author of more than a dozen books on architecture. Dr. Crosbie has written for a number of journals and magazines, including *Historic Preservation, Domus, Architectural Record, Landscape Architecture,* and *Architecture Week,* and has won several journalism awards. He is currently the Editor-in-Chief of *Faith & Form* magazine. Dr. Crosbie teaches architecture at Roger Williams University, and has lectured at architecture schools in North America and abroad. He practices with Steven Winter Associates, an architectural research and consulting firm in Norwalk, Connecticut.

Merrill Elam, FAIA, is a principal of Mack Scogin Merrill Elam Architects in Atlanta, Georgia. One of the firm's specialties is library design.

Acknowledgments

Many people were involved in the creation of this book. Thanks are extended to the architects and designers who agreed to have their projects published (and to the clients that had the foresight to build them). Special gratitude is expressed to the photographers who generously allowed use of their photographs. Merrill Elam's Introduction is an invaluable addition to this book for which I am deeply grateful. Finally, thanks to Alessina Brooks and Paul Latham of The Images Publishing Group and its staff for their support of this publication, and for bringing it to fruition.